4.95
X

The Story of Gregg Shorthand

THE STORY OF

GREGG

SHORTHAND

Based on the Writings
of John Robert Gregg

Edited by
Louis A. Leslie

GREGG DIVISION   McGRAW-HILL BOOK COMPANY

New York   Chicago   Dallas   San Francisco   Toronto   London

FOREWORD

John Robert Gregg had the most inventive and ingenious mind ever devoted to shorthand. For once, there seems to be no exaggeration in applying the word "genius" to a young man who, at the age of eighteen, had devised a shorthand system altogether different from anything previously known—the most nearly perfect shorthand alphabet yet produced. He did this while working full time in a lawyer's office between the ages of fifteen and eighteen.

Four cities may claim the honor of being important in the history of Gregg Shorthand. The system was invented in Glasgow and published, in 1888, in Liverpool. The first American edition was published in Boston in 1893; but it was not until the inventor settled in Chicago in 1895 that Gregg Shorthand began the upward drive that has continued until it is today, and has been for many years, virtually the only system taught in the United States.

This volume, as its title indicates, is *The Story of Gregg Shorthand* rather than the life of its inventor. Nevertheless, it seems pertinent here to include some information about his birthplace. The clipping containing this information was sent to the editor by an Irish correspondent living in the area in which Gregg was born, Mr. Patrick J. Creighan, of Monaghan, Ireland. The clipping is from the Northern Standard, the local newspaper, and is dated August 23, 1957.

> Plenty of information is available as to Gregg's later life, but for some time facts about his childhood were rather difficult to ascertain. His exact birthplace gave rise to the greatest speculation, and at one time it was believed that he

v

first saw the light in the Clones area. In later years it has been stated and thought that he was born at Bushford Railway Station, Rockcorry. Regarding his birthplace, however, and other interesting details, the air can now be cleared as a result of information received by our Ballybay correspondent on Tuesday of this week, when he was visited by a local resident who has his facts accurately compiled.

The interview revealed that John Robert Gregg was born in Shantonagh, Ballybay, in June, 1867. The boy's father, George Gregg, was then stationmaster at Bushford Railway Station, Rockcorry, and held the position from 1864. The family resided at Shantonagh, as there was then no living accommodation at the station. John Gregg lived at Shantonagh until he was five years of age, and the family then moved to Bushford, Rockcorry. His first day in school was at Rockcorry N.S., on 19th August, 1872. The family emigrated to Scotland in 1878, and John Gregg later travelled to Boston, U.S.A. After he invented his shorthand system, he sent one of the first books to the man then in charge of Shantonagh Railway Junction, but unfortunately this book has not been preserved. Gregg came on holidays to Ballybay district in 1939 and here met the man who has furnished these details to our correspondent. They travelled to Shantonagh, where Gregg pointed out the house where he was born.

For the record, this is a three-roomed house which is vacant at the moment but is in good condition.

In Part 2, Gregg mentions, in the first paragraph of his talk, "Rockcorry, the little country village in the north of Ireland where we lived." Our Irish correspondent informs us that Rockcorry is now part of the Irish Republic, which at the time did not exist.

The purpose of this volume is to collect some of Gregg's writings that are now out of print and not generally available. For those who were never privileged to know the inventor personally, these writings give some idea of the man and his mind. The picture these writings give is quite inadequate. He did little formal writing or talking. He was, however, a great conversationalist. The editor had the privilege of working closely with Gregg for thirty years and can never forget the many happy hours spent listening, spellbound, as Gregg shared the experiences of a rich and varied life and reading.

Readers may be interested to know that the longhand and shorthand illustrations on pages 80, 81, and 83 are in Gregg's own hand, having been photographically reproduced from a copy of *Basic Principles of Gregg Shorthand*.

One of the most important and interesting features of his life and work—"The Forward Movement"—does not appear in any part of the present volume. This is a phenomenon difficult for the present generation of shorthand writers and teachers to understand. The name is a clever play on words. It originally referred to the fact that, unlike most of the other shorthand systems of his time, Gregg Shorthand was based on the slope of longhand and therefore was written with a forward movement, without the backward-slanted characters common to the other systems.

Soon after the publication of Gregg Shorthand in Liverpool, in 1888, Gregg and his small but enthusiastic band of followers began to talk of the Forward Movement (this time with capital letters!), meaning the progress of Gregg Shorthand against the then prevailing systems.

What is so difficult for present-day shorthand writers to understand is the almost religious fervor with which the shorthand writers of that time fought tooth and nail for their respective systems. That fervor is almost totally lacking today, although even fifty years ago, when the editor of this volume first entered the shorthand field, that fervor was still strongly felt in the United States. The only quotation in this volume that gives any idea of that feeling is the one from the preface of the British edition of 1901, quoted in Part 4. If you will read that quotation aloud, remembering that every word of it was written from the heart, you will have some idea of the feeling of the time.

We hope that some day there will be a biography of John Robert Gregg that will do him justice. We hope that some day it may be possible to issue a volume of his complete writings, including his letters. In the meantime we are happy to have this opportunity to express, by the labor of love that has produced this volume, something of the great debt owed to John Robert Gregg by all those who today and in the future enjoy the fruits of his genius.

Louis A. Leslie

CONTENTS

1

THE STORY OF SHORTHAND

During the spring and early summer there had been rumors of invasion. As the great Queen sat in her palace near London on that day in July, 1588, she knew that the Spanish Armada had sailed and that the Spanish cannon would be hammering at the gates of England within the month.

History tells us how all England rose as one man to repel the invaders. The nobility gave their fortunes to build and equip warships. The commons marched and trained in every town in England. Every British sailor had his place in the fleet assembled at Plymouth under Lord Howard of Effingham—a small fleet of small ships manned and commanded by great sailors . . . Drake, Frobisher, Hawkins, Davies . . . men whose very names stir the blood today.

Yet during that frantic year of preparation not every man in England gave his whole time to thinking how to repel the Spaniard. At least one man had been giving his time to a project of special interest to every reader of this book. Timothe Bright, "Doctor of Phisicke," was working on a shorthand system, the first shorthand system of modern times, the first shorthand system since the fall of Rome.

In that perilous year of 1588, when England's fate hung in the balance, Timothe Bright invented "Characterie—An arte of shorte, swifte, and secrete writing by character."

As Elizabeth directed personally the preparations against the menace of invasion by the Spanish fleet, she did not neglect her routine duties. Barely a week before the "Invincible Armada" first sighted the "Lizard," during those last moments of peril when every anxious second was important, Elizabeth took time to grant a patent to "her well-beloved subject" for a "shorte and new kynde of writing by character to the furtherance of good learning."

There is a certain irony in the thought that this patent on the first modern shorthand system was granted by the great Queen, when it is remembered that shorthand was reserved almost exclusively for men during the first 300 years of its history. The Earl of Rosebery was overruled when he suggested to the first International Shorthand Congress in 1887 that women might some day become shorthand writers.

THE STORY OR THE HISTORY? It is more helpful to the shorthand teacher to know the story of shorthand than the history of shorthand. A knowledge of the colorful story of shorthand gives the teacher an interest in the subject that he otherwise would not have. The story of shorthand may often be useful to the shorthand teacher who will use bits of it to brighten a dull shorthand period or a blue Monday or who will use it to enlighten the academic teacher who often thinks and sometimes says that shorthand is a new subject with no background.

The Latin teacher may be reminded that the earliest surviving shorthand system was invented by Marcus Tullius Tiro, a freedman of Cicero, in order to record the orations of Cicero.

The English teacher may be reminded that some of the plays of Shakespeare were saved for us as they were pirated by shorthand writers who sat in the audience and took down the plays that might otherwise never have been preserved. The English teacher may also be reminded that the plays of George Bernard Shaw were first written by him in shorthand and transcribed by his secretary.

The history teacher may be reminded that Woodrow Wilson drafted his state papers in shorthand and often typed them himself, and that Pope Pius XII used shorthand and typing constantly.

When Cardinal Roncalli succeeded Pius XII as Pope John XXIII, one of his first acts was to present the typewriter used by Pius XII to Cardinal Montini, who had worked closely with Pope Pius for many years. Then Cardinal Montini, in turn, succeeded John XXIII as Pope Paul VI. Thus that historic typewriter has been associated with three Popes. Although Pope John gave Pope Pius's typewriter, because of its sentimental value, to Pope Paul, Pope John himself was a skilled typist and continued to use a typewriter after he became Pope.

Stories such as those and the others given in this part are more helpful and useful to the teacher than details of the hundreds of shorthand systems invented in the last 2,000 years. If such details are desired, they may be obtained from the many excellent shorthand histories that have been published—Melin in Swedish, Navarre in French, Johnen in German, Chiesa in Italian, Pitman in English. These books are seldom available, however; and when they are, linguistic difficulties render most of them inaccessible to most readers.

FOUR SHORTHAND EPOCHS. Pitman, in his *History of Shorthand*, presents an interesting hypothesis (apparently first written in 1847) concerning the epochs of shorthand history. Writing in 1963, we are able to extend that hypothesis by adding one more epoch. Pitman says:

> In reviewing the history of shorthand from its commencement to the present time, it will be obvious that the three principal epochs in the improvement and dissemination of the art, ending respectively at the times of the publication of the matured system of Mason in 1682, of Taylor in 1786, and of Phonography in 1837, may be assigned to some specific and social cause.

He points out that the shorthand advances culminating in Mason's system in 1682 "may be looked upon as resulting from the dawn of religious freedom." The second epoch, culminating in the publication of Taylor's system in 1786, according to Pitman, was due to the "dawn of political freedom" and the demand for the verbatim reports of political speeches and parliamentary debates. The third epoch, culminating in the publication of Isaac Pitman Shorthand in 1837, was caused by "the diffusion of knowledge among the middle classes of society."

The fourth epoch, culminating with the publication of Gregg Shorthand in 1888, is the epoch of the general use of shorthand for business correspondence instead of for the highly specialized work of the shorthand reporter. This is the epoch of the introduction of the typewriter and of woman's advent into the business world.

Gregg, in conversation, once called this writer's attention to the strange fact that shorthand systems seem to come in fifty-year cycles. Almost without exception every shorthand system that ever attained widespread use was published very close to a fiftieth anniversary of the first modern shorthand system. Notice how close they come to the '88s and '38s:

Bright	1588	Mavor	1789
Shelton	1641	Gabelsberger	1834
Mason	1682	Pitman	1837
Weston	1727	Gregg	1888
Taylor	1786		

Shelton's system was not only used widely in its day but it is also sure of a permanent place in history because it is the system used by Samuel Pepys in keeping his famous diary.

Perhaps the one outstanding exception is the system of Byrom (1767), but that system was never taught widely and was not published during Byrom's lifetime. It is notable as the system used by John Wesley, founder of the Methodist Church, and his brother, Charles Wesley.

Mason's shorthand system (1682) is the oldest still in use. It was appropriated almost in its entirety by Thomas Gurney and published by him in 1750. That system is still used in reporting British Parliament debates and is used by an American shorthand reporter known to the writer.

In his rare leisure moments for many years, Gregg used his great private shorthand library for research on *The Story of Shorthand*. Although he never completed the work, *Selections from the Story of Shorthand* was published in 1941 to make the material more generally available. Some interesting background material from the *Selections* is quoted in Gregg's own words in the balance of Part 1. The page references are given immediately after each excerpt.

Shorthand and the Early Christian Church

THERE is good reason to assume that St. Luke reported the Sermon on the Mount in shorthand. We know definitely that St. Paul dictated the Epistles to the Colossians to two stenographers. Many of the popes and bishops of the early Christian Church were accomplished shorthand writers.

St. Genesius of Arles suffered martyrdom rather than transcribe an edict of the Roman emperor against the Christians; consequently, there has been a movement to name him patron saint of stenographers.

St. Augustine (354-430 A.D.) employed ten stenographers, and he relates in his 141st letter that the proceedings of the great conference of 564 bishops held at the Gargilian Hot Springs, Carthage, 411 A.D., were reported by eight shorthand writers, writing alternately. In his 44th letter he states that, when some of the reporters were not willing to record his addresses to the conference, several of his adherents among the bishops volunteered to do so. No more convincing evidence could be cited, to show how widely the art of shorthand had become a part of education at this time. (*Page 1*)

The Tironian notes consisted of thousands of arbitrary signs for words and phrases. As previously mentioned, Seneca, the famous orator and philosopher, added to the Tironian notes several thousand arbitrary signs of his own invention; and St. Cyprian devised thousands of abbreviations for scriptural terms. "Thus," says Dr. J. W. Zeibig, "was the work successively advanced until it comprised no fewer than 8,000 characters—surely enough to reach the acme of perfection." We shall not attempt to comment on this conception of "perfection," and quote it merely to indicate the difficulties with which the students of the wingèd art had to contend in ancient times.

Perhaps these long lists of arbitrary signs for words and phrases were responsible for the sad fate of Cassianus when teaching shorthand. Cassianus had been Bishop of Brescia; and when he was expelled from his see, he established an academy at Imola, in the Province of Bologna, where he taught shorthand. It is recorded that one day his exasperated pupils suddenly surrounded him and stabbed him to death with their *styli,* crying as they did so, "What is it that you complain of? You yourself armed our hands when you gave us these implements—in this fashion we pay you back for the thousands of notes you taught us and, despite our tears, compelled us to learn." There is no record of the cause of their annoyance; but we hazard the conjecture that it was on a Friday afternoon, and that Cassianus had assigned a lesson of a few hundred arbitrary signs to be committed to memory by Monday morning. Fortunate, indeed, is the teacher of modern shorthand, whose students are armed only with harmless pencils, because there are times— but why pursue the subject?

But the writers of shorthand in those days had their troubles as well as the teachers of the art. Marcus Aurelius Clemens Prudentius, the most famous of the Roman Christian poets in the third century, expressed regret at the unhappy fate of a shorthand writer who was reporting a trial in court. The centurian Metellus, having been converted to Christianity, refused to perform some of his duties as a Roman soldier; he was what we should now term a "conscientious objector." Metellus asked a fellow Christian, who was a shorthand writer, to report the trial of his case. When the judge decided the case against Metellus and condemned him to death, the shorthand writer flung his tablets at the head of the judge. His subsequent fate is told in the laconic statement, "By order of the judge, he was torn to pieces."

At one time it was decreed that stenographers who copied the writings of the teachers of the doctrines of Christianity should have their hands "hewn off."

Then there is the tragic fate of the stenographer to a great ecclesiastic, who, being found dozing when he should have been transcribing his notes, was dealt such a vigorous blow on the ear that he died from the effects of it, and the churchman had to leave the city in order to avoid trial for manslaughter.

In view of the difficulty of writing with a stylus and on wax tablets, and with the crude form of shorthand then used, it would seem that the shorthand writer had enough to worry about without added burdens; but we find that in the third century the Emperor Severus—who was well named!—decreed that a shorthand writer who made a mistake in reporting a case in court should be banished from Rome and have the nerves of his fingers cut so that he could never write again! (*Pages 4-5*)

Shorthand in the Renaissance

THE first evidence we have of the revival of shorthand in the Renaissance is the fact that the sermons of the "new prophet," Girolamo Savonarola (1452-1498), were reported in some form of abbreviated writing by Lorenzo di Jacopo Violi. There are many omissions or incomplete sentences in these reports, and in parentheses this quaint explanation is made by the reporter: "Here I was unable to proceed on account of weeping." Now it is true that many of our present-day shorthand writers occasionally find themselves "unable to proceed" with the dictation, but not because of "weeping," although doubtless there are times when some of them have felt like relieving their feelings in that manner when transcribing their notes. One is inclined to believe that Violi was merely camouflaging his inability to keep pace with the fiery utterances of the great Florentine; but since all historians declare that Savonarola's sermons were so eloquent and impressive that they strung the Florentines "to heights of spiritual exaltation which they had never before or since attained," let us be charitable to Lorenzo di Jacopo Violi, who was attempting to report the great orator amid waves of emotional frenzy. Savonarola, however, acknowledged that he had been reported with accuracy. (*Page 15*)

Arbitrary Signs

THE concoction of arbitrary and fanciful signs for words and phrases exercised an almost hypnotic influence on the shorthand authors who followed John Willis, for it is evident that many of them spent much more time, and displayed vastly greater ingenuity, in devising purely arbitrary signs for words and phrases than they did in the construction of their alphabets. In the system of John Willis, *the sun* was represented by a large circle with a dot in it; *the moon* by a semicircle; *heart* by a picture of a heart; *the world* by a very large circle with a small circle in it. The idea of a large circle for *the world* was so suggestive a pictograph that it was developed by subsequent authors to the limit of its possibilities, as will be seen from the following illustrations, all of which are taken from one book:

◯	the world, worldly, worldliness	◗	low down in the world (*the other world* in some systems)
⟨•	the beginning of the world		entering or coming into the world
•⟩	the end of the world		leaving or going out of the world
⊙	in the world		through the world (*from one end of the world to the other* in some systems)
Ö	the eyes of the world		
Ȯ	upon the world	⊖	throughout the world
◎	round the world	⟝O⟞	before and after the world
♂	high up in the world (*this world* in some systems)	⊕	Christ came into the world

By that time the student had a good start in the world! It was, however, a mere beginning on the lists of arbitraries that confronted the students of those days. (*Page 26*)

Changes in Uses of Shorthand

WHEN the story of shorthand is told, a question always asked is, "What on earth did people use shorthand for in those early days?" In our time, the value of the art to everyone who has much writing to do is almost lost sight of because it has become so closely associated in the minds of most people with the work of the office amanuensis or the reporter. Fortunately for the art itself and the world at large, there are now very clear indications that this restricted view of shorthand is giving way to a broader understanding and appreciation of the enormous benefits that may be derived from a knowledge of it as a personal accomplishment and as a means of economizing time and effort in a hundred different ways.

But let us get back to the question of why shorthand was so widely studied and used by men in all walks of life during the seventeenth century. A partial explanation was given by Lord Rosebery in the course of his presidential address at the opening of the first International Shorthand Congress in 1887, when he said:

"The publication of Bright's treatise has in some respects an interesting historical origin, which is that it was in consequence of the Reformation—of the eagerness that was shown at the Reformation to take down and record the sermons that were preached and the discourses that were preached on an event which moved the nation so deeply—that the study of Shorthand was systematically and enthusiastically pursued."

A more accurate explanation would have been that, while Bright's Characterie had its inspiration in the desire to revive an art much prized by the Romans, the rapid growth of shorthand in the generation succeeding Bright was due to a realization that the art might be made use of in reporting sermons and plays, and in keeping diaries. Some remarks made by the writer in the course of an address to teachers on "The Evolution of Methods of Teaching Shorthand" seem to be apropos at this point:

It would be both interesting and instructive to have an account of the methods of giving instruction in shorthand since the modern revival of the art more than three centuries ago. Such a review would make it clear that the methods of teaching the subject, as well as the textbooks in which the art was set forth, have been influenced largely by the social, religious, political, or commercial activities of the period in which the instruction was given, or in which the textbooks were published. We should find that as modern shorthand was revived in England soon after the Reformation, at a period of great religious activity, the chief purpose for which it was studied in the seventeenth century and in the early part of the eighteenth century was to record for personal use, or to preserve in permanent form, the utterances of great preachers and divines.

Hence at that period the shorthand textbooks were filled with special signs and other abbreviations for scriptural expressions, reminding one of the statement of St. Cyprian, in the third century—at a time when the Christian religion was still battling for recognition—that he had invented 7,000 arbitrary signs for scriptural terms for the purpose of "rendering the art more useful to the faithful."

Later, when the art began to be made use of in recording court proceedings, shorthand textbooks reflected this extension of the art in the manner in which they provided special signs for law expressions. After the Gurneys were appointed official reporters for Parliament, the textbooks of the Gurney system, and of other systems, reduced the number of special forms for theological and legal terms, and introduced abbreviations for Parliamentary and political terms, and also for the phrases commonly used in speeches of all kinds. Still later, after the introduction of the typewriter, when shorthand began to be widely used in business offices, the special forms for theological, Parliamentary, and political terms were almost wholly eliminated, and those for commercial expressions took their place. (*Pages 32-33*)

Defoe, Watts, and the Wesleys

IN one edition of *Robinson Crusoe* there is an anecdote of Daniel Defoe (1659-1731) when a youth that throws an interesting light on one of the uses to which shorthand was put at that time. During the reign of Charles II it was feared that printed Bibles would be suppressed, and many people were diligently engaged in copying the Bible in shorthand. To this task Defoe applied himself with enthusiasm; and he tells that he worked like a horse until he had written out the whole of the Pentateuch, when he grew so tired of it that he was willing to risk the rest. It would be interesting to know if shorthand assisted Defoe in writing the immortal *Robinson Crusoe, Memoirs of a Cavalier*—the most real and truthful of early historical romances—*Captain Singleton,* or any of his numerous other works.

Dr. Isaac Watts (1674-1748), the composer of many of the most widely used hymns in the English language, in his book on *The Improvement of the Mind,* paid this pithy tribute to shorthand: "The art of shorthand is of excellent use for this purpose as well as other purposes." Dr. Watts was a writer of Metcalfe's Stenography (published 1635), and the Reverend W. D. Bridge notes the fact that "From his thousands of hymns the Methodist hymnal has chosen seventy-nine, whose very existence, it may be, we owe to his mastery and use of shorthand."

John Wesley (1703-1791), founder of the Methodist Church, was an accomplished shorthand writer, as was his brother, Charles. The former kept his diary in Byrom's Shorthand for more than fifty years, and the last entry in it was made on February 27, 1791. He began the diary when at Oxford, and kept it throughout his public life. At first he wrote up the diary from day to day, but as the years passed it was kept for every hour of the day, beginning sometimes at four o'clock in the morning and continuing until ten o'clock at night.

On April 8, 1749, Charles Wesley presented as a wedding gift to his bride, Sarah Gwynne, a Bible with an inscription written in shorthand. Charles Wesley was a very skillful writer of Byrom's Shorthand; indeed, his shorthand notes were so artistic that Dr. Byrom wrote him: "I shame at my own writing when I see the neatness of yours." Charles Wesley's journal, begun in America in 1736, contains page after page of the neatest and most accurate shorthand, and this is true also of his Shorthand Telemachus, his copy of the letters relating to the supernatural disturbances at Epworth Rectory, his extracts from letters received from the Countess of Huntington, and his Scripture selections. One of the most remarkable monuments of his patience and industry, as well as his skill as a shorthand writer, is a manuscript volume of the Book of Common Prayer containing the Morning and Evening Services, together with the Collects, Epistles, and Gospels for the year, and having on the last page the following inscription in his own handwriting: "Finished July 12, 1779, in a Fortnight (C.W., aged 70)."

In the early part of the eighteenth century, there was another famous clergyman who was not only a writer of shorthand but a practical reporter, Dr. Thomas Secker, Bishop of Bristol and Oxford, and afterwards Archbishop of Canterbury, to whom we are indebted for reports of the debates in the House of Lords, which he took down in shorthand from 1735 to 1743, a most eventful period in English history. (*Pages 34-36*)

Pepys and the Diary

THE most interesting diary ever published was that of Samuel Pepys (1632-1703), which was written in Shelton's Shorthand. In his *Life of Samuel Pepys,* Lord Braybrooke says that "as Pepys availed himself of his facility in writing shorthand, he was enabled to record his most secret thoughts and to note down his memoranda with clearness and dispatch." The diary began January 1, 1659, and continued for nine years, when it was discontinued on account of failing eyesight. It gives a vivid and intimate account of the court of Charles II, the political movements and intrigues of that period, the Great Plague, and the Great Fire of London; in short, all historians acknowledge that, without Pepys' Diary, it would be impossible to write an accurate history of that very interesting period.

The famous diary, after lying in the Pepysian Library, Magdalene College, Cambridge, for over 120 years after its author's death, was deciphered and published at the instance of Lord Braybrooke in the year 1825. It was transcribed by John Smith, an undergraduate of St. John's College and a reporter. "He was occupied three years at his task, usually working twelve or fourteen hours a day, with frequent wakeful nights. . . . Subsequent editions were very much enlarged with new matter and notes, but the literary public was always deceived as to the actual extent and nature of the omissions."

The Braybrooke family had always taken a deep interest in Magdalene College, of which they are patrons, and the third Lord Braybrooke discovered the Diary in the collection of books which Pepys bequeathed to the college library. A recent writer states that "it cost Lord Braybrooke three years of labor, working fourteen hours a day, to transcribe the Diary." Here we have an example—in modern times— of the master's getting credit for the work of the shorthand writer, just as Cicero was formerly credited with the invention of the shorthand system used in reporting the Roman Senate, instead of his secretary, Marcus Tullius Tiro.

That Pepys was a skillful shorthand writer is sufficiently evident from the neat and fluent manner in which the notes of the Diary are written, but there is other evidence of this in the Diary itself, for he records that, in October, 1680, he attended the King for ten days at Newmarket, on which occasion "he took down in shorthand from the King's own mouth" the narrative (which has since been frequently published) of Charles's escape after the battle of Worcester. (*Pages 41-42*)

The Famous House of Gurney

THERE was something splendidly audacious in the manner in which Thomas Gurney appropriated Mason's work, seeming to say, "I am honoring you in the taking." Doubtless it was in this lordly way that Hugh de Gourney, the Norman baron who fought under William the Conqueror at Hastings, took a goodly slice of England and became the progenitor of a family that had many distinguished members in the course of centuries. In similar fashion, Thomas Gurney, taking the alphabet of William Mason's system with but two slight changes, founded a dynasty of official shorthand reporters to the British Houses of Parliament. It must be admitted that if it had not been for the superlative professional ability and skill of Thomas Gurney and his descendants, the name of William Mason would not now occupy so prominent a place in shorthand history. The achievements of Mason's system as applied by the Gurneys focused the attention of all writers of shorthand histories upon the merits of the Mason plan.

To anyone engaged in the practical application of shorthand, the history of the House of Gurney is of absorbing interest. This great reporting firm was established by Thomas Gurney nearly two centuries ago, and the Gurneys have held the appointments of Official Shorthand Writers to the House of Commons and the House of Lords since 1813. As the Gurney system is virtually identical with that of William Mason's 1707 edition (which was a development from his earlier editions of 1672 and 1682), the system has been in use for more than two centuries and a quarter! (*Page 58*)

Between 1772 and 1786, the Gurneys published reports of a large number of trials—eleven in folio size, six in quarto, and several in octavo. When the celebrated trial of Warren Hastings began in

1789, Joseph Gurney (son of Thomas Gurney) was appointed to take verbatim notes of the evidence and speeches for the Managers representing the House of Commons. He discharged this duty personally, with but few exceptions, at every sitting (there were about 150 sittings) during the seven years the trial lasted. It was said at the time that the speeches of Sheridan and Burke were so rapidly spoken that no shorthand writer could be expected to take them verbatim, but Joseph proved equal to the occasion; his report was fully approved. His shorthand notes are still preserved and their legibility was demonstrated by the remarkable fact that, the original transcript having been lost, his notes were transcribed a second time in 1859-1860 for the Treasury; that is to say, about seventy years after the trial! (*Page 61*)

In the course of their business, the Gurneys traveled to various parts of the country, particularly to Edinburgh and Dublin. Burns's familiar warning, "A chiel's amang ye takin' notes," referred to W. B. Gurney, as did also Byron's mention of the name in "Don Juan":

> The best is that in shorthand ta'en by Gurney
> Who to Madrid on purpose took a journey.

Mr. Gurney Salter, in his brochure, says: "The Gurney staff had a peculiar character; it did not consist of shorthand writers picked up year by year, but of men who gave their lives to it. Coming into the office as young men, they began by learning to transcribe the shorthand notes of writers on the staff until they had acquired a high proficiency in writing and other qualifications required for becoming members themselves. Some men entered at about the age of twenty and continued until they passed seventy. In one instance a member of the staff had his two grandfathers, a great-uncle, his father, a brother, and three sons in the office at different times."

An interesting episode is mentioned by Mr. Gurney Salter which illustrates how the mind works automatically in the case of trained reporters:

> In the course of this enquiry, a little incident occurred which is interesting to Shorthand Writers. The House more than once sat all night, and W. B. Gurney took notes all the time. "One morning about two o'clock," he says, "Sir William Emerson gave a long description of the fortifications of Flushing. I dropped asleep, and lost myself completely. I was awoke by being called upon to read the last answer.

I said to the witness: 'I am afraid I have lost the last part of your answer. Will you watch it as I proceed?' I read on, and at the end came four lines as well written as the rest, but of which I had no recollection. He said: 'That was the whole.' How I had taken it when asleep I cannot conceive." Similar cases were mentioned at the International Shorthand Congress in 1887. (*Page 63*)

Charles Dickens and Shorthand

THERE were many accomplished writers of the Gurney system outside the Gurney staff. Among these was Charles Dickens. While Dickens achieved his fame in the field of letters, it should not be forgotten that, if he had not known shorthand, and had not practiced it in the courts, the immortal characters that abound in his works might never have been put on the printed page. Dickens' experience as a reporter in the courts, in Parliament, and on the hustings gave him an insight into many phases of human nature and furnished him with the "characters" and much of the material that he wove into his stories.

Dickens entered a lawyer's office as office boy at an early age. As his father was a shorthand reporter, Dickens decided to study shorthand. At eighteen years of age, after a varied reporting experience, he entered the gallery of the House of Commons as a Parliamentary reporter. That he was a very talented reporter is acknowledged by all his contemporaries. One of them, Thomas Beard, has stated very emphatically, "There never was such a shorthand writer." Another, James Grant, who reported alongside Dickens, said: "Among the eighty or ninety reporters, Dickens occupied the very highest rank, not merely for accuracy in reporting, but for his marvelous quickness in transcribing." Dickens himself took such pride in his achievements as a reporter that he said: "I left the reputation behind me of being the best and most rapid reporter ever known." On another occasion, after he attained world-wide fame as an author, he wrote to Wilkie Collins: "I dare say I am at this present moment the best shorthand writer in the world."

In an address at the second anniversary dinner of the Newspaper Press Fund on May 20, 1868, Charles Dickens gave this interesting account of some of his experiences as a reporter—an account that vividly portrays the difficult conditions under which he worked:

I went into the gallery of the House of Commons as a Parliamentary reporter when I was a boy not eighteen, and I left it—I can hardly believe the inexorable truth—nigh thirty years ago; and I have pursued the calling of a reporter under circumstances of which many of my brethren at home in England here—and many of my brethren's successors— can form no adequate conception. I have often transcribed for the printer from my shorthand notes important public speeches in which the strictest accuracy was required, and a mistake in which would have been to a young man severely compromising, writing on the palm of my hand by the light of a dark lantern in a post-chaise and four, galloping through a wild country, in the dead of the night, at the then surprising rate of fifteen miles an hour. The very last time I was at Exeter I strolled into the castle-yard there to identify, for the amusement of a friend, the spot on which I once "took," as we used to call it, an election speech of my noble friend Lord Russell, in the midst of a lively fight maintained by all the vagabonds in that division of the country, and under such pelting rain, that I remember two good-natured colleagues, who chanced to be at leisure, held a pocket-handkerchief over my note-book after the manner of a state canopy in an ecclesiastical procession. I have worn my knees by writing on them in the old back row of the old gallery of the old House of Commons; I have worn my feet by standing to write in a preposterous pen in the old House of Lords, where we used to be huddled like so many sheep kept in waiting till the woolsack might want re-stuffing. Returning home from excited political meetings in the country to the waiting press in London, I do verily believe I have been upset in almost every description of vehicle known in this country. I have been in my time belated on miry by-roads towards the small hours, forty or fifty miles from London, in a rickety carriage, with exhausted horses and drunken postboys, and have gotten back before publication, to be received with never-forgotten compliments by Mr. Black, in the broadest Scotch, coming from the broadest of hearts I ever knew. I mention these trivial things as an assurance to you that I never have forgotten the fascination of that old pursuit. The pleasure that I used to feel in the rapidity and dexterity of its exercise has never faded out of my breast. Whatever little cunning of hand or head I took to it or acquired in it, I have so retained as that I fully believe I could resume it tomorrow. To this present year of my life, when I sit in this hall, or where not, hearing a dull speech—the phenomenon does occur—I sometimes beguile the tedium of the moment by mentally following the speaker in the old, old way; and sometimes, if you can believe me, I even find my hand going on the tablecloth. Accept these little truths as a confirmation of . . . my interest in this old calling. (*Page 66-69*)

Evolution of Shorthand Principles

AT this point it may be well to recapitulate the development of the broad principles of shorthand construction, as distinguished from systems. The progress of the art may be summarized under twelve steps.

1. BASED ON LATIN CAPITALS. The first step was the derivation of the characters of the Tironian "notes" from the majuscules, or capital letters, of the Latin writing of that time. The minuscules, or small letters that could be joined, and that were written uniformly as in our current running hand, did not come into general use until the ninth century. As the majuscules of Latin are written in all directions—for example, *V* is written with a back-slope character and a forward upward character; *A* is written with an upward character, a back-slope character, and a horizontal crossbar; *T* is written with a horizontal and a vertical stroke—the shorthand characters derived from the majuscules were *written in all directions*—back slope, forward slope, horizontal, and vertical.

2. IMITATION OF LATIN STYLE BY MODERN AUTHORS. The second step was the imitation of the Tironian notes by the early English authors, and, consequently, the adoption of the majuscule basis, which imposed the multisloped style of shorthand writing upon the art for centuries.

3. SIMPLIFICATION OF CHARACTERS. The third step was the gradual progress, through a series of early English systems, toward the expression of each letter of the alphabet by a single character. This is probably the most clearly defined step of all.

An interesting illustration of this development is the evolution of *f* and *v*. In the Tironian notae, the letter *v* was expressed by two strokes—a back-slope stroke and a forward up-stroke—an imitation of the Latin capital *v*. Beginning with John Willis in 1602, the compound sign used by Tiro for *v* was adopted to represent that letter by E. Willis (1618), Witt (1630), Dix (1633), Mawd (1635), Shelton (1641), Metcalfe (1645), Farthing (1654), and by more than a score of other authors of early English systems. This symbol continued in use for that very purpose, and in the very form, down to and including the popular system of James Weston, published in 1727.

A forward step, in the simplification of the form for *v,* was taken in 1672 by William Mason, when he dropped the upward stroke and used only the single back-slope character. This was so brief and practical that it was adopted by the two most famous authors of the eighteenth century, John Byrom and Samuel Taylor, as well as by Macaulay, Tiffin, Lewis, Floyd, Dodge, Gould, Hinton, Moat, Sproat, Tear, and others. It should be noted that these authors, with the exception of Macaulay, Tiffin, and Floyd, expressed *f* or *v* by the *same sign,* the back-slope stroke.

With Thomas Molineux's *Abridgement of Byrom's Shorthand* (1796), still another evolutionary step was taken in the representation of this letter. Molineux said: "*F* and *v,* the latter being in general represented by the same mark as *f;* although, occasionally, it may be useful to distinguish from the former by making the stroke a little thicker." Molineux gave the same direction for distinguishing between *s* and *z,* "which were signified by one and the same line, the letter *z* being made a little thicker than the *s.*" William Harding, in his edition of the Taylor system (1823), published after the death of Taylor, adopted Molineux's expedient for distinguishing between *f* and *v* by shading the latter. He also adopted the same method of distinguishing between *s* and *z,* which were previously written alike.

Isaac Pitman studied the Harding edition of Taylor and wrote it for seven years. In the first edition of his system in 1837, *Stenographic Sound-Hand,* he used the same signs as Harding for *f* and *v*—the straight back-slope character, written light for *f* and heavy for *v.* In a later edition (1840), he changed the form to a back-slope *curve.* Thus, the representation of *v* in many modern systems is merely a modification of the form used for that letter by Tiro before the Christian era!

Other examples could be cited, but these are sufficient to show how the compound forms for letters gradually gave way to simple forms, many of which were merely modifications of the forms used in the earliest of English systems, and some of them modifications of the forms used by the Roman note-takers before the Christian era.

4. INTRODUCTION OF PHONETIC PRINCIPLE. The fourth step in the development of the principles of construction was the gradual acceptance of the principle of "writing by sound" and the provision of characters that rendered it possible to express the sounds phonet-

ically. The author of the first system of alphabetic shorthand, John Willis (1602), said: "It is to be observed that this art prescribeth the writing of words, not according to the orthography as they are written, but according to their sound as they are pronounced." As the alphabets of the early English systems—at all events, those preceding Tiffin's system in 1750—were not arranged on a phonetic basis, since they provided characters for *c* (which is sounded as *k* in *could*, or as *s* in cease), *q* (which is pronounced *kw*), *x* (which is pronounced *ks*), and did not provide characters for sounds like *sh, th, ch*, it was impossible to carry out the direction to write words "according to their sound."

Most of the early authors recognized this limitation and contented themselves with directing the student to "omit silent letters." It was not until the end of the eighteenth and the beginning of the nineteenth centuries that the statement of the principle, "omit silent letters," was changed to "write by sound," and that characters were provided that rendered it possible to carry the direction into effect—Tiffin (1750), Holdsworth and Aldridge (1766), Conen de Prépéan (1813)), Phinehas Bailey (1819), Towndrow (1831), Pitman (1837), and nearly all authors of modern systems.

5. THE PAIRING OF CONSONANTS. The fifth step was the arrangement of the consonantal characters in pairs according to their phonetic relationship; thus: *p, b; t, d, etc.*—by Holdsworth and Aldridge (1766), Conen de Prépéan (1813), Byrom (1767), Pitman (1837), and others. The genesis of the plan by which the letters were paired, in Molineux's "Abridgement of Byrom's Shorthand," has been previously explained.

6. ADOPTION OF FACILE CHARACTERS FOR VOWELS. The sixth step in the development of shorthand construction was a very slow and halting one. It was toward the expression of the vowels by more facile forms than were assigned to them in the older systems. In the earlier systems the expression of vowels by strokes was so clumsy that it is not surprising that some of the early shorthand authors (Samuel Taylor, for example) went to the other extreme of omitting them, or at most expressing any vowel by a dot. This plan, in time, resulted in attempts to provide more definite expression of the vowels by dots and dashes.

Mr. Harding, in his "Rules for Writing," said: "A vowel may occasionally be inserted in the middle of a word . . . the first vowel after the consonant may be distinguished by striking the consonant from the vowel's place; *a* may be considered above the line; *ei* on the line; *ou* below the line: but in the hurry of following a speaker, it cannot possibly be attended to. Some of these Rules are only given for beginners. The principal difficulty which young persons experience is, the omission of the vowels."

In those leisurely days, when shorthand was studied for the most part by highly educated and studious persons as a useful accomplishment, or was studied over a series of years by a few persons for professional reporting, the absence of vowels was not so keenly felt as in our day. After much laborious practice, well-educated persons and trained reporters could sometimes tell instinctively when it was wise to insert a vowel; or, if a vowel were omitted, they could often determine from the context, or from memory, what the word should be, even when the "consonantal skeleton" represented a dozen words.

In more recent times, when shorthand has been studied for the most part by young persons for use in business, the ridiculous mistakes that have been made on account of the omission of vowels in the shorthand forms have emphasized the importance of a more adequate expression of them. Young writers do not have the education, discrimination, or maturity of judgment necessary to enable them to "guess" correctly which word out of a possible dozen or more represented by the same "consonantal skeleton" was dictated. It was this factor, more than any other, that gave vitality to the demand for a more definite expression of the vowels than had prevailed. It became obvious that if the vowels were to be incorporated in the outline, they should be represented by the smallest and most facile characters; otherwise, the frequency of the vowels would render the word forms lengthy and ungainly.

This idea was felicitously expressed by Mr. Duran Kimball:

"Consonants are to a word what the bones are to the body—the large, strong framework. Vowels are to words what the flesh is to the body: they give to them form, flexibility, volume. It is desirable that two classes of sound should be represented by letters readily distinguishable; to the consonants should be assigned large letters, and it is best that the vowels should be represented by small letters."

In harmony with this reasoning, circles and hooks were eventually adopted for the representation of vowels—Stackhouse (1760), Blanchard (1786), Conen de Prépéan (1813), Aimé-Paris, Duployé, and others. It was difficult for authors of English systems who had been accustomed to the omission of the vowels to forego the use of circles and hooks to represent—at least as alternative signs for the alphabetic characters—frequent consonantal sounds such as *s, r, l*. Many authors attempted to retain the circles and hooks for consonants and to use joined ticks, dashes, and even strokes for the vowels, producing systems in which the writing was extremely ugly and lengthy.

7. ALLOCATION OF CIRCLES AND HOOKS ACCORDING TO VALUES OF SOUNDS AND SIGNS. The seventh step was the recognition of the fact that, if the smallest and most facile signs—circles and hooks—were used to express vowels, they should be allocated in accordance with the comparative frequency of the vowels and the comparative facility of circles, small and large, and of hooks.

Following the lead of Stackhouse (1760), nearly all the authors of joined-vowel systems, in which circles and hooks were used to express vowels allocated the most facile of the signs—the small circle— to *a,* and the next most facile sign—the large circle—to *o,* and the less facile hook to *e,* although *e* was manifestly much more frequently used than *a* or *o*. Doubtless, the use of the large circle for *o* was suggested by its resemblance to the longhand *o* without regard to its facility or frequency value. This unscientific allocation of the material applied also to the hooks. The study of longhand motion disclosed the fact that the undermotion used in writing the letter *u* in longhand was more facile than the upward motion used in writing the longhand *n;* but this point had been disregarded in the allocation of the vowel signs in most joined-vowel systems.

It should be noted, however, that it was only with the appearance of systems based on the longhand slope, in which the vowels were represented by circles and hooks, that any attention was paid to the teachings of longhand as a guide for evaluating the comparative ease with which various characters are written. As long as the geometric style prevailed, the facility values of hooks in various directions did not receive serious consideration.

The history of vowel representation may be summarized as follows:

Under "Disjoined Vowels," we might trace the use of the disjoined signs for vowels, beginning with the dot for *i* in Rich (1646); then the use of "commas" as well as dots, Mavor (1780); and the gradual substitution of dashes for "commas"; the placing of dots in different positions with relation to the consonants—at first in five positions (Byrom—1720), later reduced to three; the formulation of rules governing the use of these dots and dashes before and after consonants; and the extension of the phonetic principle to the dots and dashes expressing the vowels and diphthongs.

Under "Vowel Indication," we might begin with Tiro's method of writing the characters for consonants at different angles to express vowels and trace the evolution of the expedient through Gurney's "vowel modes" (adopted, in part, by Professor Everett in 1852); through Pitman's method of indicating—in the case of a few characters only—where a vowel occurred by writing some letters upward to show that a vowel followed it and other strokes downward to show that a vowel preceded it; through Melville Bell to Pocknell, Valpy, Browne, and others who extended this expedient to *all* consonants. As all the purely "vowel-indication" systems have passed away, it is hardly necessary to discuss them. None of them did more than indicate *where* a vowel occurred; and any method that does not indicate not only where a vowel occurs but also what the vowel is, or approximately what it is, has no chance of consideration in these times.

Another attempt at vowel indication was that of writing words in various positions with relation to the line of writing. The Pitmanic systems placed words in *three* positions, each position being supposed to "indicate" that one of about five vowels or diphthongs occurred somewhere in the word. This number was extended to *five* positions (one position for each vowel of the ordinary alphabet, and the diphthongs) by J. George Cross (1878), a plan that was adopted by a number of authors—McKee, Byrne, Chartier.

Under "Joined Vowels," we might trace the evolution of joined-vowel systems from stroke forms, beginning with Tiro, on through Willis and others; the gradual substitution of simpler forms, beginning with the use of the circle by Stackhouse in 1760 and Blanchard in 1786, leading to the adoption of the circles, hooks, and loops by Conen de Prépéan (1813), Aimé-Paris, Duployé, and others as the most facile and logical material for the expression of the vowels. Later, many English and American systems readopted this principle, largely through the partial success attending the publication of adaptations of the French system of Duployé to English. Still later, with Gregg Shorthand, came the use of the circles, hooks, and ovals for the expression of the vowels in accordance with the facility value of the material and the frequency value of the vowels represented.

8. THE CURSIVE STYLE. The eighth step in the development of shorthand construction was the adoption of the elements of longhand writing, with their uniform slope.

"What is natural survives"; and we can now see that it was inevitable that, as time went on, the trend of shorthand would be away from the majuscule basis, with its multisloped characters, and towards the minuscule, or cursive, basis that embodied the natural movements of the hand in current writing. The first steps taken in that direction, however, were hesitating, and at times erratic. Even the alphabet of John Willis (1602) took a timid step in this direction in the expression of *v* by a character resembling the small *v* of current writing. Other authors extended the use of cursive characters to *r, h,* and other letters.

That forward-running characters were more facile than back-slope or vertical characters was recognized early in the history of English shorthand. This is shown by the fact that, in many of the systems published in the seventeenth century, the characters on the usual slope of longhand, or with an onward movement, were given the preference in the representation of frequently occurring letters. That the reason for the greater facility of such characters was also recognized is evident from a statement appearing in the textbook of one of the most talented of shorthand authors, John Byrom, M.A., F.R.S., when he said: "The other *th* [a back-slope character] *by reason of our customary method of learning the letters the contrary way in common writing is not so readily made.*"

Although the greater facility of characters written on the common slope of longhand was thus acknowledged, there is no evidence that any of the early authors recognized that the constant changing of direction, and of the position of the hand, was a serious obstacle to rapid writing. At all events, if recognized, it was deemed impracticable, with the limited material then available, to construct a system consisting *entirely* of characters on the longhand slope. There was, too, a natural reluctance to "sacrifice" the back-slope characters.

The first system founded wholly upon a cursive basis was that of Simon George Bordley (1787); but as it was buried in a formidable treatise called *Cadmus Britannicus,* it escaped attention. It was not until 1802, when Richard Roe published "A New System of Shorthand, in which legibility and brevity are secured upon the most natural principles, especially by the singular property of their sloping all one way according to habitual motion of the hand in common writing," that the cursive principle was stated boldly and definitely as a basic principle in the construction of a shorthand system.

Like nearly all departures in any line from old and long-established practice, the cursive theory of shorthand was generally regarded by shorthand writers as utterly impracticable. Although the principle was sound, as subsequent events demonstrated conclusively, the first attempts to give effect to it were very crude and unattractive. After the publication of the systems of Bordley in 1787, Roe in 1802, and Oxley in 1816, little attention was paid to the cursive principle in shorthand construction in England for nearly seventy years.

But in the meantime the principle had been adopted by the great German author, Gabelsberger, whose system, published in 1834, became the basis of all the German, Austrian, Italian, and Scandinavian systems. The success of the cursive style in Europe resulted in a revival of interest in England, where it had originated. The subsequent story of its world-wide adoption is known to all our readers.

9. THE MERGING OF TWO PROCESSES OF DEVELOPMENT. The ninth step was the merging of two processes of development—a momentous event the full significance of which seems to have escaped the notice of shorthand historians. As previously stated, through two centuries the trend of the alphabets of English and French systems, founded on the multisloped basis, had been toward "a simple character for a simple sound." On the other hand, the early cursive systems were founded on a close imitation of the characters of longhand, with the result that in the most successful of these systems, the German systems of Gabelsberger and Stolze, many letters required two or three strokes for their expression, as in longhand.

The writing in the German systems on the cursive basis consisted of "meandering loops and lines," and those who acknowledged the success of the German systems on the cursive basis—and also acknowledged that it was perfectly logical that shorthand should be founded on that basis—were repelled by the lengthy, involved, and inexact forms of the cursive style as expressed in the German systems. To those who were accustomed to the simple, clear-cut, definite forms of the English and French geometric systems, the appearance of the cursive style in the German systems created a very unfavorable impression. This unfavorable impression proved to be an insuperable obstacle to the introduction of adaptations of the German systems in England, France, and America, and to the success of indigenous systems founded on the German style of cursive shorthand.

The situation then was: The logic of the argument in favor of a style of shorthand written in accordance with the easy, natural, and uniform movements of ordinary writing was indisputable; and it was equally indisputable that systems founded on that principle had attained much greater success in Germany and eastern Europe, so far as the general use of shorthand was concerned, than had any or all the systems in France, England, or America, founded on the multislope, geometric basis. Admitting all this, the shorthand writers and teachers of France, England, and America were absolutely opposed to the cursive style, as expressed in the German systems, however fluent it might be, because the outlines in that style appeared so long and intricate.

The question remained: Was it not possible to combine the simple, clear-cut forms of the English, American, and French systems with the longhand-slope principle; that is, to construct a system on the longhand-slope basis, in which each simple sound given in the alphabet should be represented by a single character?

Many attempts were made to construct systems on the cursive principle with alphabets consisting of simple characters, but for nearly a century the limitations of shorthand material on the longhand slope rendered these attempts abortive. Either the alphabets contained too many letters represented by the same character, or they lacked the means of clearly expressing some important sounds. For example, Roe represented *p* and *b* by one sign, *t* and *d* by one sign, *k* and *g* by one sign, and *f* and *v* by one sign. It was only in recent times that the ideal of a simple sign for a simple sound, combined with distinctiveness, was attained in a system on the cursive basis. In our opinion the merging of these two distinct currents of shorthand development marked the greatest advance made in shorthand construction in the past century.

10. PREFERENCE GIVEN TO CURVE MOTION. The tenth step was in the direction of giving curves the preference over straight lines. In the early stages of shorthand development, it was natural that the straight lines should be regarded as the most facile material for the representation of individual letters. The oft quoted axiom, "A straight line is the shortest distance between two points," had a convincing ring about it. Consequently, for a long time, the authors of systems first allocated the straight lines to the most frequently occurring letters. Having disposed of this material to their satisfaction, they next allocated the curves to the less frequently occurring sounds—and so on. The values of individual letters and individual characters were the governing factors—little or no thought was given to the values of letters and characters *in combination with one another,* or to the fluency and flexibility of curves in forming combinations.

The result was that the writing in the older systems, in which straight lines predominated, had a stiff and angular appearance, and was executed with a jerky movement. As Mr. H. L. Callender, B.A., expressed it, "Straight lines are easy enough to write *independently,* but they are rigid and inelastic when joined to other characters."

The Preface of one of the early editions of Gregg Shorthand said:

The real strength of Gregg Shorthand lies in its alphabet; all the rest is subsidiary. In his earlier efforts at shorthand construction, the author, adhering to the precedent of his predecessors, followed the theory that the most facile characters must be assigned to the representation of the most frequent letters. He laboriously compiled statistics showing the comparative frequency of letters, or rather sounds, and devoted a great deal of time to scientific experiments with a view to determining the ease with which the various shorthand characters could be written. In these experiments the results of the investigations of others were of no value, as they had been made from a geometrical standpoint. The alphabets developed by these experiments were hopelessly inefficient, and he was, for a time, reluctantly forced to acknowledge the truth of the assertion so often made that it was impossible to construct a practical system of shorthand using the slope of longhand as a basis, and in which there should be neither shading nor position writing. When he was almost disheartened, there came to him a new idea, *that the value of a letter or a shorthand character is determined by its combination with other letters or characters.* From that idea has come a revolution in shorthand.

The assignment to individual letters, as we have said, is of slight importance; the vital matter is the use made of the combination. Realizing the importance of the discovery he had made, and the vast potentialities that lay back of it, the most exhaustive experimental investigations were made to evolve an alphabet that would endure.

11.   THE NATURAL BLENDING OF CHARACTERS.   The eleventh step was the blending of the characters in natural curve combinations, thereby almost entirely eliminating the obstructive obtuse or blunt angle, and at the same time augmenting the curvilinear tendency of the writing. This was a logical development of the principle that curve motion should be predominant. Here it should be observed that in systems written on the slope of longhand there are but two obtuse angles—those between the horizontal straight line and the upward straight line, and *vice versa*—whereas in the geometric systems there are *eight* obtuse angles between straight lines. With the introduction of the blending principle in Gregg Shorthand, even the two obtuse angles that remained in a longhand-slope system were almost entirely eliminated.

12.   ELLIPTICAL CURVES SUPERSEDE EXACT CURVES.   The twelfth step was the recognition that exact curves, whether half circles or

quarter circles—the latter usually spoken of as quadrants—were not in harmony with the elliptical, or longhand, basis of shorthand. The earlier systems for the English language, in which there was an attempt to combine the cursive style with that of "a simple stroke for a simple sound," were all by writers of the geometric style who had been "converted" to the cursive theory. When they attempted to combine the two principles of construction, they retained the geometric formation of the curves to which they had been accustomed. They accepted the cursive *principle* but failed to understand or give effect to the *spirit* of it.

That is generally the way with new inventions. Man moves forward timidly, hesitatingly, from the known and familiar, until by a series of successive steps his invention approaches perfection.

The result was that in earlier systems in which the simple stroke for a simple sound idea was combined with the longhand slope, the outlines had all the angularity of the geometric systems, without the fluency of the cursive German systems, although the forms were briefer than the latter.

We were among those who failed at first to grasp the full significance of the longhand basis of cursive shorthand so far as the forms for the curves were concerned. Like others, we thought chiefly of uniformity of slope, not fluency of writing. We had been trained in geometric shorthand, but had adopted the cursive principle with enthusiasm and then proceeded to apply it, as our predecessors had done, with a mental and physical bias toward exact curves. Our previous study and practice of Gabelsberger and Stolze, in adaptations to English, had not been thorough enough, at least in the practical application of them, to enable us to get away entirely from the geometric formation of the curves.

We understood the application of it in part, but that part was confined entirely to the horizontal curves. In our first experiments, the horizontal curves were given a sloping character—similar to the top of a longhand *n,* or the lower part of a longhand *a*—but it did not occur to us that in these horizontal curves, and in all other curves, the natural curvature should be greater at one end than at the other. The realization of this came later. As John Ruskin said, "A good curve is not uniform in curvature, but curves most at one end." The application of this principle to the curve characters has been largely responsible for the artistic beauty of the forms in Gregg Shorthand and the ease with which they are written. (*Pages 112-121*)

2

GREGG
SHORTHAND—
ITS EARLY
HISTORY

In 1913 there was a celebration in Chicago
for the silver jubilee of Gregg Shorthand. As one
of the features of that celebration, John Robert
Gregg told the story of the invention of Gregg
Shorthand. The talk was reported in shorthand
and subsequently printed. It was the privilege
of this writer to hear that story retold on many
similar occasions, including the golden jubilee
celebration in 1938. On a number of these occasions, this writer made a verbatim report of

the story in shorthand. Each time some of the incidents would be included and some of them omitted.

The writer then reviewed the transcripts of many such reports and included in one comprehensive account every episode that had been recounted on any one of the occasions. This account was then revised and approved by John Robert Gregg. The result is a fascinating and informal account of the background of that young genius who at the age of eighteen had already invented Gregg Shorthand and who at the age of twenty had published his invention.

T O begin at the very beginning, my father had a friend named Annesley, who was one of the early exponents of Pitman's Phonography. This friend came to visit my father in Rockcorry, the little country village in the north of Ireland where we lived, and went to church with my father on Sunday morning. Being a shorthand enthusiast, he took his notebook with him and began to take notes of the sermon. In that little village a stranger was always a source of interest and curiosity, and when Mr. Annesley began to take notes, you can imagine how the attention of the congregation was focused upon him.

I do not suppose that anyone in the congregation had ever seen a shorthand reporter before. The young clergyman became exceedingly embarrassed and almost broke down in his sermon. When the services were over, the young clergyman rushed down the lawn in front of the church and begged Mr. Annesley not to publish the sermon because he had taken it from some famous preacher of that time.

The event made such a great impression on my father that he insisted upon all five of his children learning shorthand. For this reason, in tracing the factors that led to my taking up shorthand, I think the story should properly date from the reporting of the sermon in that little country village by my father's friend, Mr. Annesley.

So, as they grew up, all of my three brothers and my only sister studied shorthand. My two older brothers took up the study of shorthand, but they did not seem to be particularly interested in it and failed to make any practical use of it. Then came the two brilliant children of the family, my brother George and my sister Fanny. My sister was

six years older, and George was four years older than I. My sister
Fanny went through the girls' school and was awarded the first prize
every year she was in school. George went through the boys' school
and was awarded the first prize every year he was in school with the
exception of one year when he was second. It was very monotonous
for the other children.

And then, after they had left their respective schools with these
brilliant records, I came along. The headmaster thought it was an appropriate occasion on which to call the boys together and tell them
about the achievements of my brother George and my sister Fanny.
He made an address to the assembled school in which he told about
my brother George and what he had done, and exhibited his copybooks
and exercise books, which he had kept all those years for exhibition
purposes. Then, dramatically, he pointed to the little red-headed youngster by his side and said: "Here we have another of the Greggs"—and
went on to predict an equally brilliant career for me.

Now, the truth of the matter is that my position in the class was
almost the reverse of my brother's—that is to say, I was at the bottom
of the class, except on two occasions, I believe—once when I got second from the bottom, and once when I managed to get third place
from the bottom. Very unjustly, as I think, the headmaster developed
a great prejudice against me for falsifying all his predictions. He had
a very cheerful way of hearing a recitation while he was splicing canes,
of which I believe he had the finest and most varied collection in the
world. He had flexible canes, moderately flexible canes, and excep-
tionally hard canes. While he was hearing a recitation, it was his
pleasant custom to take whipcord and wrap it around a new cane—the
whipcord being used in this way because it rendered the punishment
so much more effective when the cane was applied to the hand—that
is, the whipcord raised ridges where it struck.

After he had decorated a cane in this way, it was his custom to
swish the cane in the air to test its flexibility—all this, of course,
being wonderfully stimulating to us. Well do I remember the extraordinary fascination with which I watched the preparation of a cane,
knowing that in all probability I would act as the experimental station
in testing its qualities. Sometimes that headmaster would take my hand,
hold it firmly, and bring down the cane time and again until later in
the day I couldn't close that hand because it was swollen so much.
And in inflicting punishment he had a trick of letting the cane slip
past the tips of the fingers—just catching the edges perhaps—and

then bringing it quickly up under the back of the hand. He had studied the art of physical punishment more thoroughly, more earnestly, than he had studied pedagogy.

I should explain at this point that the reason why I was so stupid in school was that in the first class, the teacher having been called out of the room, we boys got talking, as boys will. The teacher, coming back and finding me talking to another boy, caught our heads and banged them together, and in doing that, he broke the drum of my ear, so that I suffered all through my school days from that, and I have suffered from that more or less all my life. I didn't tell them at home about it, because they had a great deal of the old Scotch covenanter theory of life. The injunction to spare the rod is to spoil the child was a religious injunction with them. I knew from past experience that if I were punished at school (that being evidence of wrongdoing on my part) it was supplemented at home even more vigorously than was the case at school. So I didn't tell them. But I suffered with this, and couldn't hear, and consequently didn't make much progress at school.

Now, that was the impression under which I grew up, that I was a hopeless dunce; and that was the impression which all of my family had about me. When I was referred to, it was always as "poor John"; whenever I said anything that sounded ordinarily intelligent, it was a subject of comment in the family circle. I grew up with the firm conviction that my life was bound to be a hopeless failure, and I say in all seriousness that it is a tragedy for a boy to grow up with that impression firmly fixed upon his mind.

Why, with that "inferiority complex," as we call it now, firmly fastened on me, did I ever strike out for myself? My family had moved to the city of Glasgow in Scotland, and one of their friends was an old man named Gilmour, whom I revere to this day. Alexander Gilmour was not an educated man, but he had a great reputation for homely but profound wisdom. Whenever he spoke, everybody listened. He spoke very seldom; but when he did, he was deliberate and positive, which may have accounted for his reputation for sagacity.

Old Sandy Gilmour always had a kind word for me, and I hung around when he visited us. One evening he spoke to me; but as I did not hear him, my brother Jared said, "Mr. Gilmour, John is dull of hearing." The old man turned around in his chair and put his hand on my shoulder and said: "Dull o'hearing, laddie, but no dull o' brain." The effect of that remark on me was extraordinary. Up to that time, no one had ever indicated that I had any gray matter whatever—quite the reverse. To have this man with his reputation for profound wisdom say that I had anything in my brain simply electrified me.

I walked out of the house and through the streets of Glasgow all athrill, walked all the way through Kelvinside Park up under the shadow of the great University, asking myself, over and over again, did he really mean it or did he say it out of kindness? Then I remembered the reputation Sandy Gilmour had for never saying anything he did not mean. From that moment I set out resolutely to carve out a career for myself without regard for the opinions others might have of me. I can truthfully say that I believe those five words—"not dull o' brain, laddie"—were responsible for whatever success I have had in life. Alec Gilmour never knew how profound an influence his words of encouragement had upon me and, through me, upon the lives of thousands of others.

Well, as a child I grew up under that impression; and as I found that all the family had studied shorthand and all of them had failed in shorthand, I determined to stick to shorthand until I should succeed. They had succeeded in everything else and failed only in that. I had failed in everything else—and I was going to succeed with shorthand, if with anything. It was my last chance!

In looking back to that time, I can now see that I must have had some glimmerings of sense even then, because I argued quite logically that if they had failed to acquire the Pitman system it was hopeless for me to attempt the mastery of it. So I took up another system because I saw it was contained in a very small pamphlet—a little book of twenty pages with four plates of shorthand written in almost microscopic size. It was a second-hand copy and was dated 1860 by the previous owner. The original price was eightpence. The system was called the Odell system, but in reality it was just a simple presentation of the system of Samuel Taylor, first published in 1786.

The accident of my deciding to study the system of Samuel Taylor is probably what determined my career in life. If I had studied Pitman Shorthand, I should probably have mastered it and accepted it as the correct theory in shorthand and continued to write it all my life. Or else I should have failed and then I should have given up shorthand as my three brothers and my sister had done. But at the age of ten I began the study of the Taylor system, and from the very first it appealed very strongly to me. Here was something that I could actually *do,* something in which I found the joy of achievement. This was the first thing I really mastered to my satisfaction.

It is a somewhat singular coincidence, by the way, that the system of shorthand first studied by Isaac Pitman happened to be the system of Samuel Taylor in an adaptation by Harding, while I studied that same system from an adaptation by Odell.

This old system of Taylor is a very fluent one; it has no shading or position writing, and it is written along the line. The forms are somewhat lengthy, but its fluency appealed to me; and when I found that I could master it and could write it successfully, I began to think that after all it might be possible for me to master the more difficult system of Pitman, which was then so popular, and which my brothers and my sister had failed to acquire. I took up the study of Pitman. It did not appeal to me because it lacked the fluency and naturalness of the Taylor. I could not reconcile myself to shading, to position writing, to different forms for the same letter.

But now shorthand had me in its grip, and I wanted to know all about the various systems. In fact, the study of shorthand, or my success with it, seemed to so quicken all my faculties that I was able to make rapid progress in other subjects which had seemed absolutely impossible to me previously.

When I was eleven years of age, the family moved to Glasgow, Scotland, and my attention was attracted to the Sloan-Duployan system, which was an adaptation to English of the French system of Duployé.

There was a great deal of propaganda for Sloan-Duployan Shorthand in Glasgow in those days. It was introduced with advertisements which stated that by devoting two hours a day to the study of it one could write 100 words a minute in four weeks. I saved my pennies until I had enough to purchase a copy of the Sloan-Duployan "Instructor" and started to study it. I still have some of my shorthand notebooks in Sloan-Duployan Shorthand, preserved through all the years that have passed. They are scorched with fire, but they have survived. Inside the cover of one there is written in my boyish writing, "Commenced 31st May, 1884" and "Finished 8th September, 1884." It contains, among other things, a course of lectures on Logic by Professor Veitch, of Glasgow University.

I have another notebook even earlier, dated December, 1883, in well-written shorthand. I mention this because it has been claimed that someone taught me the Sloan-Duployan system in 1885, and these dated notebooks are a complete refutation of that statement. In another notebook which is almost scorched to pieces—a notebook dated 1884 —is a list of my small collection of shorthand books and magazines. There is an entry alongside an American shorthand magazine, "3d.

postage to pay," and that seems to have been regarded as very hard luck for me.

I liked the Sloan-Duployan system largely on account of the fact that it had joined vowels. In that respect it seemed a great improvement on both Taylor's and Pitman's. I studied Sloan-Duployan by myself, and was getting the magazine of that system by calling on the agent and teacher of the system. He wanted to enroll me as a student, but I convinced him that that was hopeless because I knew the system very well; and besides, I didn't have any money, which seemed to him a convincing reason. I wanted to join the Sloan-Duployan Association, but the entrance fee was 2s. 6d. and that seemed pretty hopeless to me.

The Sloan-Duployan teacher told me that no one could be admitted to the Association unless he had taken a course of lessons from him, but if I would take lessons for only one month, he would arrange for me to pass the test and have the privilege of becoming a member. That inducement failing, he said, on a subsequent visit, that on account of my great interest in shorthand (I had shown him all my foreign shorthand magazines and shorthand books, and discussed systems with him) he would see that I was admitted to the Association by a sort of special dispensation.

When I was admitted as a member, I found that the other members were all preparing for a speed competition for a gold medal offered by Mr. J. M. Sloan. The agent asked me to be one of the competitors, but I declined, believing I had no earthly chance against his students, who had been trained for the competition. He agreed, but said, "Come in anyway—I want to have a good showing for the examiner. You need not turn in your paper, but it will be good practice for you." I took part, turned in my transcript, and to my astonishment won the gold medal. That was the first thing I ever won, and the competition, by a coincidence, was held on my birthday, June 17th, 1885. Somehow I had a feeling that the teacher was not very enthusiastic about a self-taught student winning against his own students.

In addition to the Sloan adaptation of the Duployan system, I mastered the Pernin adaptation, published by Mrs. H. A. Pernin, of Detroit, Michigan; and I remember that Mrs. Pernin wrote me a post card in Pernin Shorthand, offering me the agency for her system and publications. She had, of course, no idea that I was a mere boy.

Then I found what might be termed a pure adaptation of the Duployan system published in pamphlets by Jean P. A. Martin, of

Lyons, France. I corresponded in the Duployan system with Mr. Martin and with other prominent shorthand writers. Mr. Martin was a very distinguished teacher of shorthand, and I am sure that he had no idea that he was corresponding and discussing the principles of shorthand construction with a mere boy.

You will thus see that I had studied two English systems and three adaptations of the French system of Duployé; and perhaps it was natural that, with my love of shorthand, I should then wish to know something about the art in other countries.

I had recently read a very important work, Thomas Anderson's *History of Shorthand,* published in 1882, which had a very great influence in formulating my views on shorthand systems and shorthand principles. Thomas Anderson was a reporter in the law courts in Glasgow and a writer of Pitman's Shorthand. His book was the first independent history of shorthand to be published. The author presented a copy to my employer and I read it eagerly—read it again and again. I was then working in a law office,[1] but as my employer was absent from the office a good deal, there was little to do, so most of my time was devoted to the study of shorthand systems and to the attempt to evolve a system for my own use. Nearly all my evenings were spent in the great Mitchell Library of Glasgow.

In his *History of Shorthand,* Thomas Anderson, after discussing the systems used in various countries, stated what he believed were the essentials of "a good shorthand system." One essential was that there should be no shading of the characters; another that both vowels and consonants should be written in the outline as they occurred. Then, after discussing the cursive or slope-of-longhand systems of Germany, he added another essential—that all the writing should be on the slope of our common writing. That chapter in Anderson's *History* made a profound impression on me, and I studied the German systems of Gabelsberger and Stolze in adaptations to English. I cannot remember just how I obtained the books of the German systems of Gabelsberger and Stolze, but I think that I studied one of them, the Stolze, in the public library in Glasgow—that was from an adaptation by Dr. Michaelis. Afterwards I studied the Gabelsberger from an adaptation by Henry Richter.

In 1884, when I went on my holidays to Liverpool, I spent most of my time in the Picton Library there; and when a boy on his first

[1] The building at 79 West Regent Street, Glasgow, was still standing in 1951. L.A.L.

visit to a great English city spends most of his holidays in a public library, studying shorthand, I think you will agree that he must be a crank on the subject. I still have the notebook in which I copied shorthand alphabets in the library in Liverpool.

By this time I was naturally very unsettled in my shorthand convictions. Perhaps I can describe my feelings best in this way: I liked the simplicity, the lineality—that is, the horizontal flow—of the Taylor system, and of course its freedom from position writing and shading. Frankly, there was very little that I liked about the Pitman except, perhaps, its phonetic basis as distinguished from the Taylor system, which was not phonetic, and the brevity of its forms.

In both these systems I liked the clear-cut outlines, while it seemed to me that in this respect the Pitman system was superior, because you could indicate the exact vowel if necessary, whereas in the Taylor a dot stood for any vowel. In the French system of Duployé I became very enthusiastic over the insertion of the vowels in their natural order as they occurred in the word. With the German systems I thought the outlines were extremely complicated, but I was impressed with the naturalness of the slope of longhand theory, that is to say, all the characters being written like longhand.

One could not help being impressed by the fact that in Germany the geometrical style of shorthand had been swept from existence by the systems of Gabelsberger and Stolze, which were founded on the longhand slant theory. The nature of the writing is very different, though, from our writing because it consists of "wandering loops and lines," as Gabelsberger described his system.

Now, there you have the germ of the idea on which I worked— light lines, absence of shading, absence of position writing, connective vowels, and the slant of longhand. I started to work out a system of my own without any thought of ever publishing it, but merely because I found it a fascinating occupation. It was my hobby, and I wanted a system that would give me satisfaction. At that time I was about fifteen or sixteen and was employed in a law office in Glasgow. My employer was a brilliant lawyer, of a very convivial disposition, on account of which he was absent from his office a great deal, which permitted me to work for weeks at a time at the study and practice of shorthand.

Perhaps I should be grateful that my employer had such a convivial disposition, as it enabled me to pursue these studies of mine without interruption, and I made all possible use of the time at my disposal. While thus engaged, I came across an American shorthand magazine which contained reviews of other shorthand magazines, and I sent for sample copies of all those mentioned. I did not receive samples of all of them, but it happened that one of those I did receive was a copy of *Brown & Holland's Shorthand News,* published in Chicago. The date of that copy was July, 1884, and I still have that original copy, although, as it went through a fire which destroyed my school at 94 Washington Street, Chicago, in 1900, it is in a scorched and dilapidated condition. On the cover the word "News" is printed across a very *short* hand. Underneath that is printed these words, "Chicago, the Center of the Shorthand World."

In that number of *Brown & Holland's Shorthand News,* there appeared an article which I believe was largely instrumental in determining the direction in which my efforts at shorthand construction should be directed. The article, or, rather, communication, was entitled "A Morocco Shorthander," and was written by Armand Lelioux, who is described as the "Stenograph-Revisor of the French Senate." In his communication he told about the life and labors of a Dr. Thierry Mieg, whose whole life had been devoted to science, and in particular to the investigation of systems of shorthand, with a view to constructing the system of the future. The article is too long to read, but I am going to read to you part of a letter from Dr. Mieg, which is quoted in the article:

I am writing these lines, you must know it, with tears in my eyes. If I had not devoted all my leisure during my whole life, even my nights, to this infatuation of contriving the writing of the future, I should be an esteemed physician, perhaps honored with many Academic titles, and, of course, rewarded accordingly. I should now have my friends about me, instead of living alone and sorrowful in a land of savages. But in spite of this solitude, where I hoped to find much time and quiet, I progress but slowly in my work. I am the only physician and apothecary in a town of 20,000 inhabitants. That is to say, even here my stenographic labors are very frequently put off till the night. Must I, for this reason, and weary with 63 years of life, close my task hastily because you say that time is pressing? By no means! The sum of all these reflections is, patience! The time will come, and, please God, you and I will be there. Perhaps you say, "That is very fine, but I should like to see this method at last." I answer, "I am not able to show it to you before the time. Since I have sacrificed my family to an idea, to a fancy, to a folly, if you choose, can you think that I would sacrifice by imprudence the tardy benefit of so many years of labor? The imprudence would not be that a pattern was in your hands, the noblest and most honest of all, but that it should go into the hands of—who knows? Some of those plagiarists that the world is full of."

Then follows an explanation of Dr. Mieg's intended system. He has adopted the slope of the ordinary writing, which will survive, he says, as the most beautiful of all.

I was young enough to have my imagination profoundly stirred and my sympathies aroused by this article. I was especially impressed by the fact that after all these years of investigation Dr. Mieg had arrived at the same conclusions regarding the correct theory of shorthand construction that I had worked out for myself—that is, that shorthand should be founded on the slope of longhand. I was an impressionable, enthusiastic boy, and the thought of this physician away off in Morocco with the same love of shorthand as I had—who had devoted his whole life to it—who had reached the conclusions toward which I had gradually and steadily gravitated, made a tremendous impression. It is not too much to say that it absolutely determined me to work towards the construction of a system based on the natural principles embodied in longhand.

After deciding on the basic principles—upon connective vowels, light lines, longhand slant, and the absence of position writing—I began to construct the alphabet. In doing this I followed the lines of all my predecessors in one particular, by first trying to ascertain the value of each shorthand character. For instance, I would assign a certain value to each of the strokes—a hundred for this, ninety for that, fifty for another, and so on—according to how I estimated their facility of execution. That had been the plan followed by all previous shorthand constructors, and it had been the subject of a great deal of controversy; I mean controversy as to the values of the various characters.

After I had assigned certain values to the characters, I next tried to ascertain, both from the investigations of previous authors and by personal study and investigation, what were the most frequent letters of the language, that is, the most frequent sounds of the language. That is, I had to ascertain whether s was more frequent than t, whether r was more frequent than n, and so on. After I had assigned certain values to each letter, it was a simple matter to assign to the most common letter the character to which I had assigned the highest value —and so on through the entire series.

I was then in a law office, as previously mentioned, and I had become quite an expert writer of the Sloan-Duployan system. The teacher, or agent, of the Sloan-Duployan system in Glasgow became greatly interested in what I was doing; and when he learned that I was thinking of constructing a system, he offered to collaborate with me and to publish the system. He pointed out that I could not possibly hope to do it personally, as I had no money or influence, but that as he was established in business he could do so. I agreed with this, and the rather crude system developed along the lines I have indicated was published. It was known as "Script Phonography"; it was on the slope of longhand; it had connective vowels on the Duployan plan, but it had shading and position writing, and the shading was applied even to up-strokes and to small circles and hooks.

It was a crude, hurried production, but it has some elements of merit. Well, I didn't share in the rewards and was eventually cheated out of my rights. That was a real tragedy of my boyhood days, and it embittered me for a long time. But, looking back at it now, after the lapse of so many years, I can see that it was a blessing in disguise. It impelled me to go on to the completion of my ideal. The struggle that it brought, too, hardened the fibre of my nature, gave me confidence, and prepared me for still greater struggles on a broader field.

But, to go back a little, I ought to say that even when this first system was being published I was not satisfied. The fever of invention was still in me. I determined to go on until I had reached my ideal of a system in which shading and position writing would be eliminated. The origin of the blending principle is a rather interesting illustration of how a valuable principle may be developed from a mere passing suggestion. In discussing an earlier effort at shorthand construction with Mr. William Pettigrew (a well-known Glasgow man who had been prominent in the advancement of Pitman's Phonography in its early days), he strongly criticized the presence of many obtuse angles in the specimens I showed him. Then he vehemently declared that he had always maintained that the greatest weakness in the Pitman system was the presence of many obtuse angles. Taking a piece of paper, he illustrated this by joining in succession the Pitman signs for *p-k, k-p, t-oh, oh-t, p-t, t-p, k-r, r-k;* next, he ran through a similar series with the thickened letters, beginning with *b-g;* then, the same series of characters with thick and thin strokes alternating; and finally he wrote the curve and straight line combinations like *l-p, f-r* (upward *r*), *r-sh* (downward *sh*), *t-sh* (upward *sh*), *m-ch,* etc.

After each example he would say with great emphasis, "In rapid writing, those lines will run together in the form of a large curve. You can't prevent it unless you write very carefully"—and so on for at least an hour.

It was evidently a hobby with him, and he had discussed it so many times with other phonographers that he had the illustrations at his fingers' end.

I listened to his exposition with considerable deference, for I was very young at that time and Mr. Pettigrew was a man of standing in the community—a member of the City Council. But when he had finished his denunciation of the numerous obtuse angles in Pitman, I ventured to point out that the outlines in the specimens submitted to him were on the longhand slope and, therefore, there could be only *two* obtuse angles—those between the horizontal straight line and the upward straight line, and *vice versa*—while in Pitman's Shorthand there were no less than *eight* obtuse angles *between straight lines alone*. The occurrence of these eight, too, was doubled by shading (*b-g,* etc.) and tripled by alternating light and heavy characters (*b-k, k-b,* etc.).

"Well," he said, "that is an improvement, but why have them at all? Why not have alternative characters for these upward and horizontal letters so as to exclude the obtuse angles?"

After I left Mr. Pettigrew, I could not get his argument about the obtuse angles out of my mind. A little later, when the combination and curvilinear principles became fixed tenets in my shorthand creed, Mr. Pettigrew's denunciation of the obtuse angles seemed to intrude itself in every experiment. When I was happy over some arrangement of the characters for an alphabet, I would find an obtuse angle; and immediately there would flash into my mind a picture of Alderman Pettigrew leaning over the counter of his shop in Sauchiehall Street, pointing the finger of scorn at the offending angle! There were no obtuse angles in longhand—I was forced to acknowledge that—and if the "system of the future," of which I dreamed, and for which I worked, was to be the "distilled essence of our common writing," obtuse angles *must* be eliminated. There seemed no way to eliminate them except by providing alternative signs for the letters, as suggested by Mr. Pettigrew—and where were sufficient signs for alternatives to be obtained in a script-hand system? Seemingly it was an insoluble problem, and I was utterly discouraged over it.

Then, one day came this thought: if lines which join with an obtuse angle take on the appearance of large curves when the angle is obscured in rapid writing, why is it not possible to contrive combinations with that end in view? Why not arrange the horizontal and upward lines so that when they blend in the form of curves these curves shall represent very frequent combinations of letters?

I well remember the enthusiasm and the feverish energy with which I worked day and night on that idea—how I compiled table after table of all the common combinations of letters and tested each of them. I realized that it was not enough to have conceived the theory; I must apply it to the most useful purpose. The result you know.

But that was not all. This started another train of thought: should not the entire alphabet be constructed with a view to facility in *combination;* that is, should not the characters be assigned so that the most frequent combinations—not the most frequent letters—would be represented by facile joinings? In other words, the letters ought not to be assigned according to their individual values, but in accordance with their facility in joining to other letters.

With this thought in mind, I began to investigate what were the most facile *combinations* in longhand. Very speedily I saw that the downward turn of the pen was found in every vowel and in nearly all the consonants. I noted that a downward curve always preceded that downward turn, making the combination found in the Gregg character for *pr.* Clearly, that combination was extremely natural and facile. Then I asked, what does it represent in the existing systems? In the Pitman I found that it represented *ln,* only one of the forms of *ln,* by the way, which was used in the word *alone* and a few other words, all of them infrequent. In the Sloan-Duployan system and other adaptations of the Duployé, it represented merely *ws.* In Script Phonography it represented *ch-k.*

Seeing that this combination was one that was most familiar and most natural to the hand, and that it was used to so little purpose in the older systems, I became convinced that I had made an important discovery. That discovery really was this: that in the construction of systems, too little attention had hitherto been paid to the best use of the *combinations that were natural to the hand.* I need not go into all the details of the results of my investigations, as they are familiar to you in the actual practice of the system. The first assignment was the downward curve to *r* and *l,* and the curve that precedes it to *p* and *b,* thus securing graceful, facile curves for the combinations *pr, pl, br, bl.* That in itself, however, is an exceedingly important factor in the system because it provides for the representation of these letters in their natural order by one impulse of the pen, in a form, too, that gives fluency, ease, and beauty to the writing. These combinations, too, are the most valuable of what have been termed the "consonantal diphthongs."

I worked through hundreds of alphabets; I worked morning, noon, and night; I thought of little else—and then when I had finished the work and had produced the alphabet that you are using today, I absolutely lost all interest in the matter.

My brother George, whom I mentioned, had tuberculosis and had gone to New Zealand in the hope of recovering. He died there, and then my only sister was taken in the same way. During her last illness I dropped all this work, tied up the papers, including this alphabet and the first specimen I had written in it, and put them all away. I did not open that parcel for more than a year.

My sister died in June, 1887, and the family doctor recommended that I should get away from Glasgow; so I went to Liverpool, where my oldest brother, Samuel, lived. I started a shorthand school in a little room on the top floor of a building in that city. There was no elevator in the building, and there were ten flights of stairs up to that room; but when an inquirer finally got up there, he was willing to sit down and let me talk to him. I found that to be a great advantage, because I was a very nervous and diffident youngster. I started to teach that first system (Script Phonography), and I taught it successfully for a year, until I was cheated out of my rights.

Then I took up that parcel, undid it, and found the alphabet of Light-Line Phonography, as I called it then, the alphabet of the system as it is today. For over a year it had lain there, and it had never even been tested in practice except on the first short specimen to which I refer. It had been developed up to that point by successive stages.

I had gone to Liverpool in the first place because my oldest brother, Samuel, was there. He was my senior by more than twelve years, and he knew about my work on Script. I consulted him about the treatment I received, and he approved of my resigning the agency—approved of it in very emphatic terms. When I resigned, I had absolutely no idea what I would do when the agency expired at the end of two months. Then, hesitatingly, I told Sam about my early efforts to construct a Light-Line system, and how far I had gone with it, but said that I had not tested the last alphabet—that I had lost all interest in the subject after Fanny died. This conversation took place on the platform of the Exchange Station when he was waiting for a train to Formby, where he lived. After I had finished, Sam put his hand on my shoulder and said, "John, you ought to test that alphabet, but you should not publish it if it is only just as good as other systems. It must be better; in fact, it must be much better, or you would have no right to publish it." Then, as his train came in, he recited, rather dramatically, "There is a tide in the affairs of men, which taken at the flood. . . ." Sam was much addicted to quotations!

I went home to my lodgings and took out of my trunk my papers, among them that last alphabet—an alphabet I had never tested in actual writing. I proceeded to write many specimens of matter from newspapers and magazines. The writing was from the alphabet, with the exception of a few rather obvious abbreviations I improvised for common words as I went along. You can imagine the delight I felt when I found that I had pages of very fluent and beautiful-looking shorthand. Those of you who have attempted to write the system from the alphabet alone know how easily it flows along. That was the alphabet which was copyrighted in sheet form on the 29th of March, 1888, which had been compiled more than a year previously. One of the remarkable things about that alphabet is that it has remained practically unchanged in all these years. The system was published [1] in pamphlet form on the 28th of May, 1888, in an edition of five hundred copies. There are only nine copies now known to be in existence. One is in the British Museum, London; one in the Bodleian Library, Oxford; one in the National Library of Scotland; one in the Congressional Library, Washington; one in the Yale University Library. The New York Public Library had a copy, but that copy disappeared. A few are in the hands of private individuals. It was published at one shilling—twenty-four cents—and I paid $100 for a very dilapidated copy a few years ago.

It consists of twenty-eight pages; the Preface begins with this statement: "A great and increasing demand for a simple, rapid, and perfectly legible phonetic handwriting for general use has led to the invention of Light-Line Phonography, which is the outcome of years devoted to stenographic study and research." Written at the mature age of nineteen years, I really did think that I had devoted a "great many years to study and research." The Preface goes on: "The system is based on natural physiological laws, and the characters have been assigned to the various sounds after long and careful experiment."

---

[1] The building at 62 Dale Street, Liverpool, was still standing in 1951. L.A.L.

Then follows a description of the system, and the Preface concludes with this:

> In conclusion, the endeavor of the author has been to compile a system so simple as to be readily acquired by the humblest capacity, and those possessed of little leisure, and yet rapid enough to reproduce verbatim the fastest oratory. In presenting his work to the public, he asks for nothing beyond an impartial investigation, and with perfect confidence awaits the result.

I want to emphasize that "with perfect confidence awaits the result." In the attack on the system published by Isaac Pitman and Sons a year after the system was published, they made a good deal of fun of the "amusing confidence" of the "youthful author"; but I noticed that when that attack was reprinted some years later, the only change that had been made in it was the elimination of the remark about the amusing confidence of the author, from which I infer that it was not quite so "amusing" then.

That first little book was published on May 28, 1888. It was then summer time, and of course it was very difficult to secure students. My first student was a young man, Fred H. Spragg, whom I taught from separate sheet lessons and who afterwards became a very brilliant writer of the system. I have seen Mr. Spragg write the system on political speeches at 200 words a minute. The rapidity with which he acquired the system, and the high speed he attained, of course confirmed me in the belief that in addition to its simplicity and legibility the system was capable of greater speed than any system previously published.

About the same time I taught the system to a Mr. Jakeman, who had acted as my assistant in teaching Script. Mr. Jakeman became a very enthusiastic advocate and teacher of the system, and one of his sons was for some years the manager of the business of the Gregg Publishing Company in Great Britain.

My next student, I believe, was Mr. J. Carlisle McCleery, who was then an official in the Customs Department of Liverpool; and I do not believe that Gregg Shorthand would have lived—or, at all events, that I would have lived—had it not been for Mr. McCleery. He was a man of unusual ability, who had devoted a great deal of his leisure time to literature, and was then a contributor to many papers and magazines.

Mr. McCleery had always wanted to know shorthand so that he

might make use of it in his literary work; and he had tried to learn two other systems, with not very satisfactory results. At the time I published "Light-Line Phonography," he was a student of Script; but without any persuasion on my part, he immediately decided to take up the new system. In doing so he declared that he intended to reach a speed of 100 words a minute within one month; and he did attain that speed, although I should explain this by saying that this was on one-minute tests, which was then the common method of testing students. It ought to be borne in mind, too, that Mr. McCleery had previously studied other systems. Most of his time was devoted to continuous dictation practice, and he had the advantage of being a skillful penman.

At the end of another month disaster stared me in the face. My slender resources were exhausted. Just at that time, in a weekly paper known as *Tit Bits,* a paper with a circulation, I believe, of nearly half a million, there appeared a statement that a Mr. Watt, a reporter in Scotland, had written in Pitman Shorthand for forty minutes at the rate of 220 words a minute. I called Mr. McCleery's attention to it and urged him to write a letter to *Tit Bits* showing the absurdity of anyone's speaking for forty minutes at the rate of 220 words a minute in a court. He said, "I should like to help you, but it is against the ethics of literary men to write letters to the papers to which they are contributors. It might prejudice me with the editor." I pleaded with him so strongly that at last he said, "Let me have the paper and I will think it over this evening."

He wrote the letter—and that letter started the system on its way. A day or two after its appearance, I received two hundred letters making inquiries, and probably a thousand letters from all parts of the world reached me in the next month. Among the papers I lost when my office in Chicago was burned in 1900 was that correspondence in *Tit Bits* of twenty-five years ago, but once when I was in London I went to the office of *Tit Bits* and asked for the file of their paper published in 1888. From the file I copied in shorthand Mr. McCleery's letters, and I am going to give them here because I do not believe the system could have survived had they not brought the inquiries that enabled me to keep it going during that trying summer when it was first published. Besides that, I think the letters are interesting in themselves.

The first letter appeared July 21, 1888, under the heading "Quick Shorthand Writing," as follows:

To the Editor of Tit Bits.
Dear Sir:

I was so deeply interested in Messrs. Pitman's account of the reporter who wrote 220 words per minute for forty consecutive minutes that I turned up the *Phonetic Journal* of 26 May to see for myself Mr. Watt's own account of his unparalleled feat. Mr. Watt, I find, states that "the time was not noted to seconds, but I have exceeded the actual space in putting it at forty minutes." It seems a pity that the exact time was not recorded, as a few minutes either way would, of course, make a wonderful difference in the speed per minute.

I have no wish whatever to cast the shadow of a shade of suspicion on the accuracy of Mr. Watt's time-keeping. His feat stands unsurpassed in the chronicles of shorthand. I cannot, however, repress a gurgle of admiration for the lung and tongue power of the Scotch Counsel which enabled the said Counsel to give utterance to 220 words per minute for forty minutes. My mother-in-law in her most excited moments couldn't come within miles of it.

As an illustration of the Counsel's speed, I may state that Messrs. Pitman's letter to *Tit Bits* consisted of 237 words. I *read* it aloud as quickly as I could, and the reading occupied exactly seventy-two seconds, or at the rate of 197 words per minute. I could not possibly have continued reading at the same rate for a quarter of an hour. A counsel who could collect his thoughts and speak at the rate of 220 words per minute for forty minutes when I could only read at the rate of 197 must indeed be an oratorical express.

Pitman's system may be all its inventor claims for it, but I don't think that many of its writers will ever reach 220 words per minute. Years ago I tried Pitman, and after six months' study managed to reach the frightful speed of 60 words per minute. Not long since, I ventured in the study of Script Phonography. After three months' constant work, I reached the speed of 80 words per minute.

Now in my green old age, I have actually started to study "Light-Line Phonography"—a system invented by Mr. John Robert Gregg, of Liverpool. After a month's study of "Light-Line" I was able to write 100 words per minute. Who knows but that some day or other I may even be able to report a Scotch Counsel!

Yours faithfully,
Whyte Tighe,
Seaforth.

"Whyte Tighe" was the pen name under which Mr. McCleery wrote for the magazines. In answer to this letter there appeared a long communication from a gentleman writing under the name "Phonographer." It ended, however, with this interesting statement:

> As one who has been a practical writer of Pitman's system for eighteen years, and who has examined every system of shorthand of any note that has appeared in this country for the last ten years, I venture to state that while there may not be *many* writers of Pitman's who will ever reach 220 words per minute, there never will be *one* who will attain to a speed of even 200 words per minute by the aid of Light-Line Phonography.

The correspondence developed, and of course the interest in the system developed also. In answer to the attack of "Phonographer," Mr. McCleery wrote a very interesting letter. After a few preliminary remarks, he said:

> Secondly, Phonographer himself acknowledges that a very rapid rate of utterance cannot be kept up for any length of time. He said he read my letter in 95 seconds at the rate of 269 words a minute, and that afterwards he read for ten minutes from one of Gladstone's speeches at the rate of 237 words a minute. In other words, he dropped 31 words in speech every eight and a half minutes. Assuming then that he continues reading for forty minutes losing 31 words in speech every eight and a half minutes, he would, at the end of forty minutes, be reading at the rate of 113 words per minute. To apply this test to the speech of the Scotch Counsel: The Scotch Counsel, to give an average of 220 words a minute for forty minutes, would have started at the child-like speed of 280 words a minute (speaking, not reading, remember) and would have finished at the rate of 160 words a minute. That Scotch Counsel for rapidity of utterance beats any bookmaker I ever saw on a race course, and the speed of the speech makes the new train service from London to Edinburgh look foolish. Had the speech been committed to one of Edison's latest machines, I wouldn't have cared to have been handy when the thing burst.
>
> Thirdly, while I won't attempt to deny that Phonographer can read at the rate of 237 words a minute, I would ask him if he has ever known any one—barring his mother-in-law and the Scotch Counsel—who could speak at the rate of 220 words a minute for forty consecutive minutes. I confess I never have.
>
> Fourthly, it will be well for Phonographer to remember that writers of the Pitman system of eighteen years are apt to bestow a very cursory examination on new methods. They

are content to believe that a system invented in the days of rush-lights and crinolines cannot possibly be improved upon. As I have mastered both Pitman and Light-Line, Phonographer must confess I have authority when speaking of the merits or demerits of either.

Fifth, Phonographer winds up by saying that while there may not be many writers of Pitman who can write 220 words a minute there never will be one who will attain to even a speed of 200 words a minute by the aid of Light-Line. Phonographer, never prophesy unless you know! Light-Line has only been in existence a few months, and I contend that it is impossible for any one yet to know what the ultimate possible speed of that system may be. I might tell Phonographer, however, that I know one gentleman who started Light-Line on May 11 who the other night wrote 161 words per minute. So, you see, Phonographer, one never knows.

Faithfully yours,
Whyte Tighe

I have given these letters simply because that discussion was the starting point of the progress of the system and because I have a great feeling of gratitude to the late J. Carlisle McCleery, whose last editorial article, published after his death in the paper he edited, *The Insurance, Banking, and Financial Review,* of London, was a tribute to Gregg Shorthand and to his experience as one of my students.

I have a very grateful feeling not only for the encouragement Mr. McCleery gave me at that time, but for the brilliant and disinterested way in which he championed the system when it was in its infancy. He was indeed a friend in need.

Another remarkable student whom I had during the first few months was a Mr. Edward J. Deason. He wrote me inquiring about the system, and a correspondence developed. Mr. Deason, after some time, told me that he believed Gregg Shorthand was more rapid than any other system and he wanted to demonstrate this by attaining a reporting speed. So I urged Mr. Deason to come to Liverpool and study under my direction. What was my surprise when I came to my little office one morning to find waiting for me a very tall gentleman with a long black beard, who proved to be Mr. Deason.

He was a very remarkable student, and one of the most remarkable characters I have ever known. A few years previously he had made a visit to this country and had learned telegraphy at a college in Janesville, Wisconsin. After learning telegraphy, he was engaged in newspaper work and, he told me, he was selected as one of the reporters for the Associated Press, or whatever the news distributing bureau of that time was called, to follow Mr. Blaine in his campaign for the presidency. Deason didn't know shorthand at that time, and as he had to report somewhat fully, he wrote abbreviated longhand.

In explaining his quickness in attaining speed in shorthand, he attributed it largely to the power of concentration he had developed in the practice of reporting in abbreviated longhand. He would never hold up the dictation, but when the speed was beyond him he would put down the important words, the "nouns and verbs," as he constantly expressed it. As I had only two or three students in the daytime I had plenty of time to devote to Mr. Deason, and he was a willing worker. On Sundays he would report sermons, always trying to attend churches where there were speakers who were more rapid than he could write. The result was that at the end of nine or ten months Mr. Deason wrote in a public hall before Pitman examiners at the rate of 200 words a minute on solid matter for six and three-quarter minutes, at which point the dictator broke down. In some respects Mr. Deason was the most remarkable writer I have ever seen.

The record was absolutely genuine in every respect, and it was one of the things that has made me so positive about the speed possibilities of Gregg Shorthand. I saw it written at over 200 words a minute repeatedly by Mr. Deason, and on one or two occasions by Mr. Spragg, when the system was in its infancy and when its outlines were longer than they are today. That was one reason why I always maintained the speed possibilities of the system and predicted the results that have been accomplished in the past few years. I was acting on the old maxim of Hosea Bigelow, "Never prophesy unless you know." I *knew*.

The trouble is that after the first year or two I became immersed in the struggle for bare existence. When I emerged from that struggle, in the multitudinous details of building up an organization, a long time passed before I had the time or opportunity to train anyone to demonstrate what the system could do in the way of speed. Besides, it is not often that you can get people who are willing to devote their time to the attainment of high speed.

I will pass over the intervening struggles and go on to the time when I decided to come to this country. The system was making wonderful progress in England. We had schools teaching it in several cities. Our records of results accomplished were splendid, and I was building up a very good business in teaching the system in Liverpool when my hearing collapsed. For six months I could hardly hear a sound, and consequently my teaching business almost vanished. About the end of that time, when my hearing was partially restored, I received a letter from Mr. Frank Rutherford, who had learned the system in England, stating that he intended to teach the system in Boston, where he was then located, and urging me to copyright the system in America.

It had always been my intention to come to this country. I was saturated with American literature, was subscribing for American newspapers, particularly the weekly edition of that unique publication of that time, the *Detroit Free Press*. I reveled in the stories and articles in that paper written by the late Robert Barr, who then wrote under the name of "Luke Sharp," as well as those of "M. Quad" and others. In fact, I was so interested in those stories and used them so much in dictation after I started my school that I believe I could now from memory dictate some of those stories almost word for word. Sometimes when people comment on the quickness with which I adapted myself to the conditions in this country, I tell them that I was half American before I came.

It appalled me to think that I was in danger of losing my copyrights in America, which I had always looked forward to as offering the greatest opportunities for the recognition of the system. I immediately prepared a revision of the entire system, sold my school in Liverpool for forty pounds—about two hundred dollars—and started for Boston.

I sailed from Glasgow because I had gone home to bid good-bye to my family. I paid four pounds for passage on the "Nestorian," which literally rolled all the way across the Atlantic, taking three weeks for the trip. During the three weeks on the ocean, I became friendly with two Scottish boys on the boat—Girvan and Mackie—to whom I gave shorthand lessons each day. Their destination was Fitchburg, Massachusetts. As soon as they reached Fitchburg, they started a class in Light-Line Phonography—which was actually the first Gregg Shorthand class in America.

The "Nestorian" finally arrived in Boston harbor on August 21, 1893. It was a Sunday night and we couldn't land, although, of course, all of us were very impatient to get off the boat.

The next morning I didn't land very promptly because the immigration inspectors were suspicious of me. My home was listed as Liverpool, but I had sailed from Glasgow. I had paid only four pounds—twenty dollars—for my fare, but I had all of $130 with me. I must be an embezzler. Finally, however, they released me.

I had this $130 left when I landed in Boston; and, of course, when I had printed the little pamphlet containing the first American edition of the system, there was nothing left. It was at this time that I changed the title of the system from *Light-Line Phonography* to *Gregg's Shorthand*. Later, I got tired being called Mr. Greggs, and dropped the apostrophe and *s*.

It was then August and the year was 1893. I emphasize that date, although perhaps few will now remember that that was the year of a great panic. Boston suffered perhaps more than any other place in the country, and I arrived there at a time when half the typewriters in that city were covered and the stenographers out of employment; when they were serving soup in the City Hall to the poor people. It was a terrible year to start anything new, especially in business education.

Mr. Rutherford's "school" was a desk in a room in the Equitable Building. He had a roll-top desk which he rented for twelve dollars a month, and he taught the students on the slides of the desk, a student at each slide. The students came for lessons by appointments, an hour constituting a lesson, with about half an hour for typewriting. To teach typewriting, he had rented a typewriter for three dollars a month, and after school hours—that is, after three o'clock—this typewriter was used by the man from whom he had rented the office, who paid three dollars and a half a month for it in the afternoon; that is, Rutherford rented it from the typewriter company for three dollars and subrented it, so to speak, in the afternoons for three dollars and a half to our landlord, which I think is a good example of high finance.

When I came, another roll-top desk was added, for which I paid an additional twelve dollars. To be perfectly frank about it, I really didn't pay the money, I simply owed it; but the good-natured old German who rented the office had a kindly feeling for us and gave us credit. I remember how, when I finally did pay off my obligations to him, he put his hand on my shoulder and urged me to keep the money for a while longer, as he didn't need it.

The old German was in the fertilizer business. He used to write long two-page form letters that were all one long rambling sentence connected with *and* and *but*. He had me type out his letters for him when I wasn't busy with pupils.

One weekend I took one of those letters home with me and worked over it all day Sunday. It was hard work, but I made a good letter out of it. On Monday I took it to the old man and showed it to him. Then I went back quietly to my desk to wait for the applause and appreciation. The old German came to me and said: "That's a nice letter, a wonderful letter; but I wouldn't send that out, because if I sent that letter out the farmers would think I am a city slicker and wouldn't buy."

I wish I could describe that room to you. There were about eight or ten "firms" doing business in it, each having a roll-top desk. Some of the important firms had two desks—we were among the important ones! The man over in the corner opposite us was an elderly gentleman who conducted a real estate business. Most of the day he slept peacefully in his chair, as the real estate business was not very brisk in those days. Whenever things were dull with us—which was a chronic condition—he would come over and read us some poetry he had written describing the lots which he had for sale. The lots, I understand, were located in a swamp somewhere outside Boston.

He had a curious sense of humor, that old gentleman. Once he described to us how he had taken a prospective purchaser to the lots; he had gone past the station to the place so that he might approach it by driving from a place where there was a more attractive view of it, and finally got the man to the place. He kept talking to his prospective customer until the man had waded almost up to his knees, and then the customer said, "Well, where is this Grand Boulevard?" The real estate man replied, "Why, this is it." I am not going to repeat the language used by the prospective customer.

I must say that that real estate man had very beautiful plans and pictures of his lots. He explained to me that he drew up the plan and then proceeded to sell the lots around the depot and the post office. After he had sold these lots, he moved the post office and the depot on his plans and started all over again.

I had very interesting experiences in watching the people come and go in that office. There was a jewelry firm, I remember, that operated for a few weeks and then disappeared, just a day before the detectives came in to inquire about them.

Those were the surroundings, and that was the environment, in which we started our campaign. The work was conducted with those two roll-top desks. On looking back at it now, it is a marvel to me that we were able to get any students. But we did get students, and very good students, and we even enrolled practical writers and teachers of other systems.

I remember that on Saturday afternoons a lady from Salem used to come in for lessons. She was dressed in her bicycle costume, the bicycle craze being at its height at that time; and after she had had about twelve lessons, she told us that she was a teacher of shorthand in the Salem Commercial School. She had been sent by Miss Emma A. Tibbetts, who was then the proprietor of the Salem Commercial School, to test the system, but had not told us this until she had made up her mind as to whether or not the system had any merit.

She was an enthusiastic teacher and advocate of the Isaac Pitman system and at first did not take to our system with any enthusiasm, but she did not say very much about it. She became very enthusiastic as the lessons proceeded, and the result was that Gregg Shorthand was adopted in the Salem Commercial School. Miss Tibbetts was therefore the first school proprietor in America to adopt Gregg Shorthand, and Miss Smith was the first teacher of shorthand to change to our system.

I have always regarded that as a remarkable thing, that these two ladies had the enterprise and independence to take such a radical step when there was so little evidence on behalf of the system, and when it did not have any organization or any textbook worth the name. It subjected them to a good deal of ridicule at first, but I think they have since had a great deal of satisfaction in seeing so many hundreds of teachers and school proprietors follow their lead.

The Equitable Building closed at six o'clock in the evening; and in order to find work evenings, I conducted a class at the Boys' Institute of Industry. I was paid $1 a night for three hours' instruction and had classes twice a week. That helped a lot.

That Institute consisted of two or three small stores which had been made over into a kind of refuge for newsboys and others. It was established with the idea of bringing the boys in off the street and giving them something useful to do in the evenings. The boys were free to select their own studies. They could take wood carving, carpentry, shorthand, typewriting—anything they liked—and there was no possibility of maintaining discipline. The idea of the founder of the school was that boys should be absolutely free from restraint and that they should feel that it was a place where they could do as they liked.

It was one of the most interesting experiences of my life to teach those boys. When a boy didn't like the study, he walked out of the class and took up something else. When he didn't like another boy, he pulled him off his chair and pounded him on the floor. When they didn't like things in general, they upset the trestle tables on which they were working, and sometimes there was a free-for-all fight. A teacher couldn't do anything except use moral suasion, that is, talk to them.

There was one boy in that class who was particularly obstreperous. I took him aside one evening and talked to him in a fatherly way, and finally he said, "All right, professor, I will help you." He lived up to his word, because the next day he had washed his face to start with, and when another boy made an interruption, he promptly pulled him off the chair and pounded his head on the floor. He was going to help the teacher all he could.

One night as I stepped out of that superheated room—it was heated by a large stove—I found the thermometer had gone down to ten degrees below zero. The wind off the bay was terrific, and the result was that I nearly died on the way to my room. I was so frost-bitten that almost the whole side of my face came off afterwards. Naturally my enthusiasm for that class languished, and I never went back.

It has been one of the regrets of my life that I did not do so, because about eight or ten years afterwards when I visited Boston, some of my old students gave me a reception, and at the end of the line was a fine-looking young man of about twenty-three. He said, "Mr. Gregg, you don't remember me?" "Well," I said, "it is so long since I have been in Boston that some of my students have grown up." "Well," he said, "I am the boy in your class at the Boys' Institute whom you talked to once." It seemed that he had become interested in shorthand and typewriting and in spelling, and he went on with those studies by himself after I deserted the class. A lawyer gave him a position as office boy, and from that he went on up. He told me that in that week he was to receive a sheepskin as a lawyer.

I had classes in various Y.M.C.A.'s all around Boston. I taught a lot of those classes free because they would buy those books—50 cents for the first pamphlet and $1 for the other.

At that time I was offered business positions, but I always refused them. I was a fanatic, a shorthand fanatic. I believed with all my heart and soul in the work and its usefulness to young people, and therefore I refused the positions that were offered me. I have starved, actually starved, for days, and I remember a pathetic entry on one page of my diary—".05 this morning, that's all."

I remember once I weakened. I had struggled and struggled, and I was sick and weary and hungry; so I went to my office and wrote a letter to a publishing company offering them my work for $200 provided that I would have the books I would want to carry on the work. I wanted to carry on the work even if I didn't make anything. Now, I knew of only two American publishers—Harper and Scribner. Harper was publishing the Munson Shorthand, so I wrote to Scribner. I outlined the merits of my system and enclosed the evidence, the testimonials, and so on, and then outlined the program of future publications that would be needed to carry on. That was a good letter.

But I never heard from Scribner's, luckily, and I struggled along.

One evening almost twenty years later at the National Arts Club (I was President or Vice-President at that time), we had some great celebration and numerous noted guests. I escorted one of them, Mr. Charles Scribner, to a seat on the dais. As we walked in, he said to me (now that was about 1915 or something like that), "Mr. Gregg, I'm very glad to meet you. We publishers have been talking a good deal about you, but none of us has met you." Of course, I hadn't met the publishers at that time, and I asked, "Why are you talking about me?"

"Well," he said, "we're talking about you largely because we happen to know that you have paid the highest income tax of any publisher in New York." I asked, "How did you find that out?"

"We have our ways of finding out," he said, "will you tell me when we sit down just how you made your start, how you achieved so much?"

"Well, Mr. Scribner, I owe it largely to your company." So I told him. He said, "What did we write you?" I said that fortunately I didn't get any answer, and I added, "Well, if I knew the man that put my letter in the wastebasket (I had a suspicion that he was the one), I'd give him the best dinner that was ever given to anyone in New York." I still think he did it himself.

No Christmas that I have ever had in my life will stick in my memory like that first Christmas Day in Boston in 1893. As Christmas approached, business dwindled to the vanishing point—you all know how students drop off at that time of the year. Now, Christmas is the

day of days in the old country, and Rutherford and I determined
that we were going to do the best we could to have one good Christmas
dinner. We summed up our joint capital and found that it amounted
to one dollar and thirty cents. There was no possibility of getting any
more anywhere.

Late on Christmas morning we walked down to a hotel—walked
to save carfare—and had our dinner, after carefully estimating the
cost from the bill of fare. I should like to have a transcript of our
conversation over that dinner. We drew a picture of the United States
covered with schools teaching Gregg Shorthand, we pledged each other's
health, we stood up and shook hands over it and vowed to continue
with this thing in which we believed with all our hearts and souls
until we had relieved the young people the world over from the drudgery
of learning the old systems.

In figuring over the meal, we had reserved ten cents for carfare
home—we had not thought of any supper. But the waiter helped me
on with my overcoat—and away went the ten cents. We trudged home
through the snow, and then Rutherford, who had a wife and family
in England, played "Home, Sweet Home" and other cheerful airs on
an old organ until we almost wept. Then we went to bed sufficiently
sad. That was our first Christmas Day, and I shall never forget it.

But that dream has come true, those things we vowed to do have
been done, and the work is going on.

In December, 1895, two years later, I went to Chicago. This
time I had a good deal of capital—I had all of seventy-five dollars
and I started a school there. I hunted around until I found the cheapest
office, an office at 94 Washington Street, at fifteen dollars a month.
I remember that I bought all the furniture for twenty-six dollars and
rented a typewriter at five dollars a month. Unfortunately, I was not
able to subrent it to someone else, as Rutherford had done with his
Yost.

The first day I put a small advertisement in one of the papers,
but I did not have much hope for callers for a few days. Within one
hour of opening the office in the morning, I had my first caller. He
found me with my coat off busy polishing up the furniture. This caller
was a gentleman who had visited nearly all the schools and was carrying
their catalogs under his arm. He said that he had a son who had a
great disinclination to study anything, and he wanted a school that
would give him a great deal of personal attention. Oh, how eloquently
I talked to him! I told him that I would be a father to that boy, that

I would devote all my time and thoughts to him, and the result was that he paid me fifty dollars for the course.

I can assure you that I honestly earned that fifty dollars. He was a big fat boy who brought a full pie with him every day. At every interval he ate a chunk of pie and then went to sleep. Finally, however, I was successful, and today he is a well-known insurance man in Chicago.

Two years later, in 1898, I was able to publish the system in book form for the first time, and the system began to move forward more and more rapidly. In 1900 it began to sweep all over the country.

Up to that time I was simply an enthusiast and didn't have much knowledge of business. When I got into the atmosphere of Chicago, I realized that it was only through a knowledge of business methods that I could accomplish the object I had in view. I learned business methods by hard study and then proceeded to build up the business organization which has done so much to spread the system. Right here I feel that I should pay a tribute to the very loyal work that has been done by those who have been associated with me in the business, and to the great help that I have had in all directions from the teachers and writers who have believed in the system and who have unselfishly recommended it whenever they had an opportunity.

3

BASIC PRINCIPLES OF GREGG SHORTHAND

In 1913 the inventor of Gregg Shorthand told the story of the personal incidents that led to his invention of the system. That account, with some added material, is given in Part 2 of this volume. In 1923 he published *Basic Principles of Gregg Shorthand*, a detailed account of the mental processes from which came the finest shorthand alphabet ever invented. When that account was written, there were still many schools teaching Pitman Shorthand in the United States. He wrote that account, therefore, with many references to the peculiarities of systems with which American shorthand teachers are no longer familiar. In recent years teachers have failed to appreciate that fascinating story of the invention of Gregg Shorthand because of the frequent puzzling references to long-forgotten shorthand systems.

In this part, the editor has excerpted the essence of *Basic Principles of Gregg Shorthand*, giving only the part that is of significance to the shorthand teacher today. No word has been changed. The excisions have been made carefully to avoid changing the sense of any part of the narrative. The original chapter headings have been retained, although a number of the chapters are omitted completely. The material that is given, is given in the same order and in the same words in which it appears in the original book.

Every teacher of Gregg Shorthand will be interested to have the account in the inventor's own words of the steps by which he developed the greatest shorthand alphabet yet invented in 2,000 years of shorthand history.

Curvilinear Motion

Motion in curves is more beautiful than that in straight lines, both because of the greater beauty of the curved line and because curvilinear motion indicates less effort.

—Dr. Francis Wayland

A good curve is not uniform in curvature, but curves most near one end.

—John Ruskin

In closing the preceding chapter I said that my next talk would be about "the most important element of either longhand or shorthand."

That element is the *predominance of curve motion*. This feature is probably the most radical departure from the older lines of shorthand construction to be found in the system. Curiously enough, its importance has not been fully appreciated by many writers and teachers, although, when the system was first published, many shorthand authors and others interested in the scientific aspect of shorthand recognized it to be an extremely radical step.

A NEW IDEA. The distinguished French shorthand author and reporter, M. Jean P. A. Martin, of Lyons, wrote me under date of June 24, 1888—less than a month after the publication of "Light-Line Phonography," as Gregg Shorthand was then called—and the very day he received a copy of my first book:

> The postman has brought me your book this morning. . . . I can but think well of a system that embodies all the ideas defended by me time and again, and is mainly constructed after the principles laid down by Conen de Prépéan, the real founder of continental shorthand.
>
> There is, however, a point that is quite new to me; I mean the predominance given by you to curve motion. Whilst Mr. Clément Gourju in his Semiographie, and Mrs. De Wik Potel in her Dewikagraphie, endeavored to do away with all consonantal curves, whilst *nearly* all of us have criticized large curves (I say the large ones, and not the *small* ones), you have taken an opposite view of the case.
>
> I am glad you have, because I have no doubt you will soon produce reporters, and their notes will be of value to shorthand scientists. We shall better be able to form an opinion on the advisability of predominant curve motion in shorthand writing. We shall watch your progress with great interest. We look upon your system as a very valuable experiment. You are the exponent of an idea, and we love *ideas* when they are carried into actual practice. . . .
>
> I shall ever be glad to give my support to men who fight for the supremacy of the sound principles established by Conen de Prépéan. It is not because your shorthand principles are French; it is because they are scientific, and Science knows no borders, no nationalities; it is human."

Writing me again on July 30, 1888, M. Martin said:

> We do everything we can in order to diminish the number of curves in our representation. You do *the very reverse:* you remove nearly all the straight lines from the consonantal alphabet. The point at issue must be settled through experience, through practice. You now understand why Shorthand Scientists are anxious to see the notes of several Light-Line Phonographers written at a speed of over 120 words a minute. They want to know what will be the effect of the

predominant curve motion on a page of shorthand. Of course, there is no question about this or that system; we do not care about systems. Scientifically speaking, we study ideas, principles, and see what results they yield, no matter the alphabet. And I can but repeat what I said before: yours is a new idea. Light-Line Phonography is, in our opinion, a very valuable experiment which all persons who are studying the Science of Shorthand cannot fail to watch with great interest.

At this point it may be interesting to quote what I said on this subject in the Preface to the *first edition* of "Light-Line Phonography," in describing the "main features" of the system:

The Predominance of Curve Motion

Curves, the prevailing element of ordinary penmanship, being more facile than straight lines, the author has, so far as is compatible with a well-balanced alphabet, assigned to them the representation of the most frequently recurring consonants. In addition to this, the straight characters have been so arranged that the most frequently recurring combinations of letters form an *obtuse* angle at their point of junction, and such angle not being observed, the letters are allowed to coalesce naturally in the form of a large curve; thus curve motion has its rightful preponderance, the maximum of facility obtainable from this source is secured, and the system is freed from the unnatural zig-zag motion of the ordinary shorthand.

This is expressed in somewhat pretentious language—I was very young then!—but it shows that recognition of the prevalence of curves in longhand writing was an important factor in the construction of the system.

In my earlier experiments at shorthand construction I followed the beaten path. The result was an *angular* style of writing—a truly "script-geometric style," as someone described it. This realization that curvilinear motion was the greatest of all the elements of longhand writing placed me on the path which led to "Light-Line Phonography," and it is the feature of the system to which, more than to any other, is due its wonderful success.

THE COMBINATION PRINCIPLE. Those who have read the "Story of Gregg Shorthand" as told at the Silver Jubilee meetings will remember the emphasis placed upon the discovery of the *combination* principle, as distinguished from the assignment of characters to the letters in accordance with their *individual* values. The successful working out of the combination principle depended upon a scientific analysis and utilization of the curvilinear motion of longhand, beginning with the ellipse or oval as a basis.

The assignment of the characters according to *individual values* in the older systems naturally and inevitably resulted in the straight lines being given the preference, as stated in the letters from M. Jean P. A. Martin, which I have quoted. Straight lines *when joined* resulted in a jerky, angular style of writing.

Joined Vowels

EVOLUTION OF JOINED VOWELS. The evolution of joined-vowel representation toward a natural and facile plan is one of the most interesting things in shorthand history. In a previous article some extracts were given from a letter written to me soon after the publication of "Light-Line Phonography" by the distinguished French shorthand author and scientist, M. Jean P. A. Martin, of Lyons. It will be remembered that Monsieur Martin commented on the radical departure from all previous theories of shorthand construction which I had made in giving the preference to curves over straight lines, and that he described "Light-Line" as being "mainly constructed after the principles laid down by Conen de Prépéan, the real founder of continental shorthand."

As I did not know anything about Conen de Prépéan at that time, I asked Monsieur Martin who he was and what were the "principles laid down" by him. Monsieur Martin's answer to my query is so interesting that I am going to quote it somewhat fully. In doing so, however, I must caution the reader not to accept unreservedly his statement that the plan of expressing the vowels by circles and hooks originated with Conen de Prépéan. His very natural enthusiasm for the achievements of a compatriot inclined my gifted correspondent to give Conen de Prépéan more credit than was actually due him.

Much as I dislike to deprive a French author of the glory of originating this method of expressing the vowels, simple justice to earlier English authors compels me to say that circles and hooks were used to express vowels before Conen de Prépéan's time. Stackhouse,

in 1760, used circles to express vowels—a small circle for *a* and a
large circle for *o, which is the very use made of them by Conen de
Prépéan, Aimé-Paris, Emile Duployé and nearly all the other French
authors of joined-vowel systems since that time.*

This method of using the small circle and the large circle has
been adopted by several English and American systems. Blanchard,
in 1786, used the small circle for *a* and *o,* and a large circle for *w.*
Holdsworth and Aldridge, in their "Natural Shorthand," published in
1766, used a small circle for *o,* a large circle for *ow,* a small loop for
eu, and a large loop for *wh.* Oxley (1816) used a downward hook for
u; and other early English authors made use of hooks for different
vowels. Undoubtedly Monsieur Martin was not aware of these facts
at the time he wrote me, any more than I was.

ALL HONOR TO FRANCE. Credit may be freely and gratefully
given Conen de Prépéan, and to Aimé-Paris, Duployé, and the other
French authors who followed his lead, for developing the principle of
using circles and hooks for vowels, and for demonstrating its superiority
to all other methods of vowel representation. It is possible, too, that
they made the best use of that material for expressing the vowels in
the French language, although I cannot speak on that subject from
personal knowledge. When I come to the discussion of the use of the
circles and hooks, I intend to show that the authors of adaptations of
the French systems to English, and of systems for English which have
copied the French vowel method, have all made a very serious mistake
in adopting the French arrangement of the vowels.

THE NOBLE WORK OF M. DE PRÉPÉAN. With these preliminary
remarks, I present Monsieur Martin's very interesting story of Conen
de Prépéan:

> Conen de Prépéan published several systems, some of
> which are still in use in the French Parliament; his alphabets
> were widely different from one another. Well, his systems
> are nigh forgotten, but his ideas and principles survived
> this unfortunate scientist who died in misery after a life
> spent over shorthand researches and experiments. Five of
> these principles are quoted, page 42 "Cours de Sténographie
> Française" by L. P. Guénin, edited by C. Delegrave, Paris.
> In fact, Conen de Prépéan is the originator of the connec-
> tive vowel systems as they now stand. Without Conen, it
> is very likely that neither Duployé nor Sloan, nor you, nor
> anybody else, chiefly in England *where Taylor reigned,* could

write any efficient system. The principles set forth by Conen
look so natural, *so simple,* so self-evident that no shorthand
author, no modern author, I mean, will ever dream, can
ever dream of building a connective-vowel system upon
other principles; Conen hit the nail on the head; unknow-
ingly, unwittingly, as all others, you and I and all of us have
adopted them. You have received them through Sloan, Sloan
through Duployé, Duployé through Aimé-Paris, Aimé-Paris
through Conen de Prépéan. They are no news now, they
are common property, everybody applies them among the
connective-vowel shorthand authors and pays as little attention to how they came about as a child thinks of the origina-
tors or inventors of our Roman alphabet. Yet what a step
from ideographic writing to Roman letter writing! What a
tremendous advance! One might say, European civilization
is the outcome of the 25 or 26 letters of the alphabet. The
alphabet is the greatest invention, the greatest blessing, and
a boy of ten does not see in it anything particular; it is so
common. The same thing occurs with Conen de Prépéan's
principles, the importance of which is not realized nowadays.

When Conen de Prépéan set to work he had before him
two systems: Taylor's, which ignored vowels entirely, and
Coulon de Thévenot's. Coulon de Thévenot wrote all the
vowels; only the syllables were disconnected, each syllable,
though very fluent, very linear, even compact was very
complicated; no connection could possibly occur among
the various syllables; it was a clumsy-looking system. Every
modern shorthand writer swears that it is impracticable
because it does look so. Yet as it was in some respects
founded on science (fluent, linear, compact enough), it is
a well-known fact that very efficient verbatim stenographers
used it with great success in spite of its bad looks: Coulon
de Thévenot *looks* a tremendously huge thing. The point,
then, was to make each syllable *very short,* and at the same
time find out a way to retain the vowels and connect each
element of the word. Taylor's system was there; what signs
on earth could be added to his alphabet? He had given the
problem up himself by dropping the vowels altogether. Other
people look to dots and accents; but that was cutting the
Gordian knot instead of untying it. The vowels were a
perfect puzzle. Of course, in older systems they were used,
but the vowel was a *complication.* Gurney, for instance, has
the following connective signs for his vowels:

[Here Monsieur Martin gave some of the illustrations
of the compound signs used by Gurney.]

Syllables were not short! and connecting was occasionally a very tough matter with the old alphabet that had kept special strokes for the vowels.

Bertin-Taylor's disciples could show very brief outlines, and Conen de Prépéan did not wish to double these in length to add the vowels. *That was a very hard nut to crack.*

Then Conen said: Let the vowel signs be *four times shorter* than consonantal ones; that'll make a difference. Then let us take circles or loops, fractions of a small circle, and ticks as vowel signs. Yes; but Taylor's consonantal signs were *not* single strokes; some of them consisted of a hook or a circle and a stroke to represent *one* letter only; the new loops and fractions of a circle would clash with the hooks of the consonantal signs. *That was another puzzle.* Shorthand materials were limited in number. . . .

Besides, supposing that there should be no clashing between the loops and hooks, the parts and parcels of the consonantal signs and the vowel signs themselves, the outlines would at any rate be long enough. What should he do?

Then Conen said: In order to represent each consonant by a *simple* sign, let us classify consonants phonetically and if *p* is short let it be the rule that the corresponding consonant *b* should be written long. So the problem of *one sign* for *each sound* was solved.

Again, the problem of devising connective-vowel systems of shorthand was solved, in *giving the vowels a form and size corresponding to their importance when compared to the consonants.*

I have not related here all we owe to Conen de Prépéan; but if you have had patience enough to follow my explanation, you cannot help remarking that the principles of that man seem now so self-evident that nobody thinks of them; yet a hundred years ago Gurney, in supplying vowel signs, could not find his way out of *bee* otherwise than by an awkward combination of strokes for both vowels and consonants. In those days nobody, except Taylor, had yet found a way to use decent connective signs; Taylor was radical: *he did not* mention them, that's all; some did the same, I believe, before him. Pitman is but a disciple and modifier of Taylor.

After this Conen was plagiarized extensively, went on working for all his life, spent a fortune, died a destitute and unhappy man, and is now forgotten. He is a true martyr of Shorthand. Whenever I see a new connective-vowel system I think of the poor fellow. What a sad thing!

Excuse haste, bad writing; I am half asleep as it is near three o'clock and the morn is near, but I wanted to answer the letter of a brother in shorthand pursuits.

OUR EARLY ACKNOWLEDGMENT. When I received this letter from Monsieur Martin in 1888, I was preparing a pamphlet entitled "Shorthand for the Million," and I took advantage of the opportunity to make this acknowledgment to Conen de Prépéan:

> Circles, hooks, and loops have been adopted as the material suitable for the representation of the vowels. This principle was first laid down by M. Conen de Prépéan, and has been adopted by nearly all the authors of modern connective-vowel systems as the most natural and effective method. It is only in the assignment of this material that most connective-vowel schemes differ, and experience proves that in this respect "LIGHT-LINE" has a very decided advantage over all the plans hitherto published. The most facile signs have been carefully assigned to the representation of the most frequently occurring vowels and vice versa, hence there is a far larger percentage of vowels inserted in rapid writing than in any other method.

At that time I was not aware that Stackhouse, Blanchard, Oxley, and other English authors had anticipated Conen de Prépéan to some extent in the use of the circles and hooks for the expression of the vowels.

A Résumé of the Seven Basic Principles

> *The development of Phonography affords another illustration of the general rule that the simplest, most convenient, and most reasonable way of doing anything is usually the last to come, but when the right thing is accepted, it seems amazing that the inferior and imperfect one could have been tolerated, much less loved and tenaciously adhered to.*
> —Benn Pitman

You will have noticed that in the preceding chapters I have discussed broad, basic principles only. An understanding of the value, and of the relative importance of these basic principles, is a necessary preliminary to an explanation of the manner in which I attempted to construct a system in harmony with them.

A RECAPITULATION. Let me refresh your memory at this point by a brief recapitulation of the seven great basic principles, which were discussed in previous articles:

1. *Based on the ellipse or oval—on the slope of longhand*
2. *Curvilinear motion*
3. *Elimination of obtuse angles by natural blending of lines*
4. *Joined vowels*
5. *One thickness—elimination of shading*
6. *One position—elimination of "position writing"*
7. *Lineality—the easy, continuous flow of the writing along the line*

All these principles are in accordance with the teaching and practice of ordinary writing; all of them are natural writing principles. Gregg Shorthand was the first system in which they had *all* been incorporated.

ANDERSON'S "FIVE AXIOMS." Mr. Thomas Anderson, author of "The History of Shorthand," in an address on "The True Theory of Shorthand," delivered before the Shorthand Society, London, March 7, 1882 (six years prior to the publication of "Light-Line Phonography"), said:

I shall not limit myself to a dry dissertation on the defects of the existing systems or an exposition of the illogical basis on which they repose; . . . but it is my design to propound, to illustrate, and to defend, what, it appears to me, are the necessary and indispensable conditions which regulate and apparently restrain the attainment of excellence in the framing and accomplishment of any modern system of shorthand. . . .

Let me, gentlemen, invite your attention to the following proposition, which I venture to submit to your consideration in the light of Shorthand Axioms. They are these:

First. The alphabet of a good shorthand system must include independent characters for the vowels, which characters must be adapted for writing in union with the forms for the consonants; in other words, every letter of the common alphabet must have a special and distinctive shorthand mark.

Second. The characters of a good shorthand system must be all written on the one slope.

Third. In a good shorthand system no distinction of letters made thick from letters made thin is admissible.

Fourth. In a good shorthand system there must be only one line of writing.

Fifth. The rules of abbreviation in a good system of shorthand must be few, comprehensive, and sure.

Permit me to point out that these five traits, according to the presence or absence of which I respectfully ask that we should assess the value of any and all shorthand—these five traits, I say, *although they have never been found combined in any single system, have yet been recognized separately by various authors, and some of them by one and others by another.*

It will be seen that all of these "Five Traits" are to be found in our system.

Several years ago, while I was still actively engaged in teaching, I telephoned to a very expert writer of the system—a man who had been engaged in highly technical shorthand work for several years —and asked him to substitute for me with an evening class of beginners. He consented to do so. The next day he came in to find out why I had introduced the diacritical marks to distinguish the shades of vowel sound. When I told him that they had always been a part of the system, he was absolutely incredulous; and, in order to convince him, I had to show him the early editions of the system. Then he remarked with emphasis, "Well, perhaps I did learn them, but I have never used them and have never felt the need of them, although for years I have been doing very technical shorthand work with a firm of chemical manufacturers."

The Evaluation of the Sounds

THE next step is to ascertain the comparative *values* of the various sounds as shown by their frequency of occurrence.

One of the claims put forth by authors of the earlier shorthand systems, as expressed by one of them, was that "the alphabet is founded on the allocation of the most facile signs to the most frequently recurring consonants." The same thought, expressed in slightly different language, occurs in nearly all the textbooks of the older shorthand systems. It would seem to be a very strong and a very reasonable position to take. But it ignores one very important fact: that the *individual* value of a sign may be greatly affected by the frequency with which it is joined to some other sign or signs.

THE COMBINATION IDEA. In speaking of the construction of the alphabet in the Preface to one of the editions of the Gregg Shorthand Manual, I referred to this theory as follows:

> The real strength of Gregg Shorthand lies in its alphabet; all the rest is subsidiary. In his earlier efforts at shorthand construction, the author, adhering to the precedent of his predecessors, followed the false theory that the most facile characters must be assigned to the representation of the most frequent letters. He laboriously compiled statistics showing the comparative frequency of letters, or rather sounds, and devoted a great deal of time to scientific experiments with a view to determining the ease with which the various shorthand characters could be written. In these experiments the results of the investigations of others were of no value, as they had been made from a geometrical standpoint. The alphabets developed by these experiments were hopelessly inefficient; and he was, for a time, reluctantly forced to acknowledge the truth of the assertion so often made that it was impossible to construct a practical system of shorthand using the slope of longhand as a basis, and in which there should be neither shading nor position writing. When he was almost disheartened, there came to him a new idea, *that the value of a letter or a shorthand character is determined by its combination with other letters or characters.* From that idea has come a revolution in shorthand.
>
> The assignment to individual letters, as we have said, is of slight importance; the vital matter is the use made of the combination. Realizing the importance of the discovery he had made, and the vast potentialities that lay back of it, the most exhaustive experimental investigations were made to evolve an alphabet that would endure. The alphabet of Gregg Shorthand has therefore been worked out on scientific principles deduced from a close analytical study of the combinations in the language and the movements used in ordinary writing.
>
> It is almost needless to say that a faulty allotment of the alphabetic characters would have entirely nullified in practice the value of the natural principles which form the basis of the system.

THE FREQUENCY OF THE CONSONANTS. I am sorry to say that the many tables on the frequency of letters and of combinations of letters which I compiled when engaged on the construction of the system were lost in the fire which destroyed my offices in Chicago in 1900. In planning this series I intended to make a new analysis and present the results, but it has been impossible for me to find time to do so. In any event, I believe that the figures given by other authors will be more effective than anything which I might personally submit.

MR. LEWIS'S TABLE.   In 1815 Mr. James Henry Lewis gave the values of the consonants in this order:

s, t, n, h, r, l, d, f, m, w, g, y, p, b, v, k, j, q, x, z.

The figures compiled by the authors of the early English systems are not of much value now, as they were based on the ordinary spelling, instead of the phonetic sounds. It will be quite apparent that *h,* for instance, which is placed fourth in Mr. Lewis's list, would be very near the end of the list in an analysis on a phonetic basis: it would be very greatly reduced in value by including it in *sh, ch, th, wh,* and through *ph* being expressed by *f;* and its value would be still further reduced by its omission in words like *honor, laugh,* etc., in which it is silent.

The great value placed upon *h* by the early authors is probably responsible for the extraordinary consideration with which that unimportant letter is treated in Isaac Pitman's Shorthand, in having no less than four methods of representation assigned to it! As mentioned previously, Isaac Pitman had written the old Taylor system for seven years before attempting to construct an improvement on it; and to this day the compound sign used for *h* in the Taylor system—a circle attached to a downward, oblique stroke—survives in the Isaac Pitman system as one of the four ways in which *h* is expressed.

The value assigned to *w, g,* and *k,* in the Lewis table would also be affected by a change from an alphabetic to a phonetic basis; *w* as a part of *wh; g* as a part of *ng* and *gh; k* as a part of *x* (*ks*), and so on.

ISAAC PITMAN'S TABLE.   In an address on "The Science of Shorthand," delivered before The Shorthand Society, London, in 1884 (printed in the *Phonetic Journal,* 12 July, 1884, and *Shorthand,* Vol. II., No. 17), Isaac Pitman said:

> I took the *Leisure Hour* for 1873, containing a variety of papers by various writers, and counted the occurrence of the letters or sounds in the first line of fifty-five columns. The experiment carried my calculation to a little over one hundred for the most frequent sounds. If I had pursued the subject to the extent of one thousand, the results would not have been different, for they agree with all my experience as a writer of shorthand. . . . The frequency of the letters is in this order, ranging from 110 to 0:

r 110, *s* 102, *t* 97, *n* 86, *p* 72, *l* 48, *k* 46, *f* 41, *m* 31, *th* 24, *sh* 17, *w* 13, *h* 11, *ng* 7, *y* 0.

Unfortunately, the report of his address does not mention *b, d, v, g, j, z;* so this table of values is not complete, but from an article by Mr. Pitman in his *Phonotypic Journal,* September, 1843, we are able to obtain more complete data. The article was entitled, "On Phonetic Printing," and was for the purpose of setting forth one of his many plans for a scheme of phonetic type to supersede the letters used in ordinary printing. He said the figures were obtained by counting the sounds in "The Vision of Mirza" (*Spectator,* No. 159), and were as follows:

n 429, *t* 422, *r* 384, *d* 334, *s* 282, *th* (as in *that*) 276, *l* 205, *z* 189, *m* 183, *v* 146, *h* 136, *p* 135, *k* 125, *f* 106, *b* 97, *ng* 74, *ch* 49, *sh* 40, *th* (as in *thin*) 39, *j* 34, *zh* 7. (Total sounds, 3731.)

It will be seen that this table of occurrences differs very materially from the one given forty-one years later. For instance, *s* is relegated to fifth place—below *d!*—and *r* is reduced from first to third place. Perhaps this is due to the nature of the articles selected—and in both instances the articles were very short.

MR. GUEST'S TABLE. In the Preface to his "Compendious Shorthand," Mr. Edwin Guest, in 1883, gave the letters on a phonetic basis in this order:

s, t, n, r, l, m, d, k, w, f, p, b, x, v, g, j, z, y, q.

Mr. Guest did not mention *h, sh, ch, th, ng.*

MR. LOCKETT'S TABLE. About the same time Mr. A. B. Lockett gave them as follows:

s, t, n, r, l, d, k, m, p, w, f, b, g, v, sh, ch, ng, j, y.

Mr. Lockett omitted *h, th, w, z.*

Omitting the letter *h* (for the reasons already explained) from the Lewis table, it will be seen that Lewis, Guest, and Lockett are in absolute accord as to the order of frequency of the first four consonants—*s, t, n, r.* In 1884 Isaac Pitman placed *r* first, but he gave the other letters in the same order as Lewis, Guest, and Lockett; in 1843 he placed *n* first, followed by *t, r, d.*

MR. CROSS'S TABLE.   Mr. J. George Cross, author of " Eclectic Shorthand," in 1892, gave the following table based on an analysis of 3000 words:

> *n* 163, *r* 144, *t* 137, *s* 85, *z* 81, *d* 80, *th* 80, *l* 76, *m* 67,
> *b* 53, *k* 52, *p* 40, *v* 37, *f* 36, *h* 24, *g* 22, *w* 22, *j* 18, *ch* 16,
> *y* 12, *sh* 11, *wh* 5, *ng* 4, *zh* 3, *x* 1.

It is important to remember that Mr. Cross's system is partly orthographic and partly phonetic. Some of the figures given by Mr. Cross are surprising; particularly those regarding *s, z,* and *th.*

MR. LINDSLEY'S TABLE.   In 1885 Mr. D. P. Lindsley, author of "Takigrafy," published a very interesting table which he said had been prepared by Mr. H. T. Beach from a careful analysis of twelve selections from different authors, each selection containing about 450 words. "The number of words in the twelve selections was 5,452; the entire number of sounds used in expressing them, 12,943, making an average of three and seven hundred sixty-five thousandths sounds to the word."

> *t* 1477, *r* 1460, *n* 1449, *s* 1007, *d* 893, *l* 857, *th* 747,
> *z* 578, *m* 555, *k* 503, *v* 440, *w* 430, *p* 407, *h* 403, *f* 388,
> *b* 343, *ng* 199, *g* 164, *sh* 157, *y* 143, *ch* 127, *th* (*ith*) 107,
> *j* 102, *zh* 7.
>
> *Note:* *wh* is given as 86; but it is stated that it should be eliminated, since it is also included under *w* and *h,* respectively.

Mr. Guest seems to have made the most careful investigation of any of the authors mentioned, and I am therefore going to quote what he said on the subject:

> The author found a general consensus of opinion among inventors that the most frequently used letters should have the easiest lines, but the analysis of their alphabets constantly revealed the strangest departures from the principle enunciated. The frequency of letters and the facility of lines were equally matters of guess, to a certain extent, of if any attempts were made to ascertain either, they were made in so unscientific a manner as to be scarcely worthy of attention.
>
> The present writer was therefore compelled to resort to the laborious process of actual counting to obtain his data.

Short extracts from Shakespeare, Bacon, Locke, Milton, Addison, Dr. Johnson, Hazlitt, Macaulay, Carlyle, Ruskin, and Kingsley; and passages from the speeches of Canning, Shiel, Lord Beaconsfield, Lord Derby, Dean Stanley, Mr. Bright, Mr. Gladstone, and other orators were counted; poetry, prose, religion, history, politics, ethics, and science all being represented; with the result that in 10,000 words (*and, of,* and *the* being left out because these common words have in most systems special marks) *s* was found to recur 2,886 times, *t* 2,700 times, *n* 2,543 times, *r* 2,175 times, *l* 1,316 times, and so forth down to *j, ch, y,* and *q,* which recurred only 198, 177, 168, and 33 times, respectively. The necessary equations having been made on account of *ks* representing *x; ph, f,* etc., the proportionate recurrences of the consonants stand thus: *s* 100, *t* 95, *n* 90, *r* 74, *l* 46, *m* 41, *d* 40, *th* 33, *k* 26, *w* 25, *f* 25, etc., down to *j* 7, *ch* 6, *y* 6, and *q* 1. Thus, *s, t, n, r,* occur 359 times in the aggregate to *j, ch, y, q,* 20 times. Hence there is an obvious advantage in giving to the first four the best possible lines and in making the last four wait until all the rest have been accommodated.

HOW "PAIRING" AFFECTS VALUES. In considering these tables, it is important to keep in mind that where the letters are arranged in phonetic pairs—*p, b; t, d;* etc.—and are represented by the same character (distinguished either by thickness or by length) their importance is increased or decreased in exact ratio to the *combined frequency of both letters.* For example, the consonant *s,* which is given first place in three of the above tables, has a very unimportant cognate, *z,* while *t* has for its cognate, *d,* which is placed fourth in one table, sixth in two of the tables, and seventh in another; and *r,* which in our system and in many others, has as a cognate *l,* is placed fifth in four of the tables, and seventh in one table.

It seems strange that, in all tables that I have mentioned, this very important factor in the evaluation of the sounds appears to have received no consideration.

THE APPLICATION OF MR. GUEST'S FIGURES. Applying this principle to Mr. Guest's evaluation of the individual letters, we get some interesting results; thus:

	Total
t 95; *d* 40	135
n 90; *m* 41	131
r 74; *l* 46	120
s 100; *z* (say) 5	105

With these figures before you, it will be interesting to see what bearing they have on certain important features in our system.

Lineality: The great importance of a lineal, continuous movement was set forth in a previous chapter. According to Mr. Guest, the letters *n, m, r, l,* which are represented by horizontal characters in our system, total 251. To these add *k* and *g*. Since *k* is valued at 26, and as *g* is placed by Mr. Guest after *f,* which he values at 25, and ahead of *j* which he values at 7, we may assume his valuation of it to be about 15, making a total for *k* and *g* of 41. The total for horizontal letters is thus 292. (This total would be further increased by the inclusion of *ng, nk,* which keep close to the horizontal.)

Balance: Another important element in shorthand construction is the preservation of an equable balance between upward and downward characters. Applying Mr. Guest's figures to the letters represented in our system by upward and downward characters, we get some interesting results.

The letters represented by *downward* characters are:

	Total
s 100; *z* (say) 5	105
f 25; *v* (say) 5	30
j 7; *ch* 6; *sh* (say) 10	23
p 12; *b* 8	20
	178

The letters represented by *upward* characters are:

	Total
t 95; *d* 40	135
th	33
	168

It will be seen from this that there is an almost perfect balance in our system between upward and downward characters; and by comparing these figures with those given for the horizontal characters, it will be seen that *the horizontal characters almost equal the combined total of upward and downward characters.*

In reality the very slight advantage for the downward characters is more apparent than real, on account of the minute size of *s*. It should be remembered that *t* and *d,* although classed as upward characters, are *onward*, forward characters; and that *t*, which has *more than double the frequency value of d,* is a *very short* upward character.

Another factor in making for both *balance* and *lineality* is the frequency with which *t* and *d* are used at the end of words after downward characters, particularly in forming the past tense. The outlines for the following words will illustrate this and will suggest innumerable other examples: *smashed, reached, pledged, alleged, raved, saved, leaped, bribed, peeped.*

The Cross and Lindsley tables are more complete than the others, and they give actual figures for all the sounds or letters. Lindsley's table is based on a purely phonetic analysis of 5,452 words; and Cross's is based on an analysis—mainly phonetic—of 3,000 words.

THE APPLICATION OF MR. LINDSLEY'S FIGURES. Mr. Lindsley's values, when the letters are paired, are as follows:

	Total
t 1477; *d* 893	2370
r 1460; *l* 857	2317
n 1449; *m* 555	2004
s 1007; *z* 578	1585
th 747; *th* 107	854
f 388; *v* 440	828
p 407; *b* 343	750
k 503; *g* 164	667
sh 157; *ch* 127; *j* 102; *zh* 7	393

Lineality: Based on Mr. Lindsley's table, the horizontal characters in our system—*n, m, r, l, k, g*—total 4,988.

Balance: The downward characters—*s, z, f, v, p, b, sh, zh, ch, j*—total 3,556. The upward characters—*t, d, th*—total 3,224.

A comparison of these figures with those of Mr. Guest will reveal remarkably close *net results.* Mr. Lindsley's figures illustrate the almost perfect balance between upward and downward characters in our system, even when the figures are based on an analysis of 12,943 sounds, occurring in 5,452 words. What we have said about the onward character of *t* and *d* (although they are classed as upward characters) should be kept in mind; and also the fact that *s* and *z* are expressed by a *very short* downward character.

THE APPLICATION OF MR. PITMAN'S FIGURES. Isaac Pitman's values, in his 1843 article, show the following results when the letters are paired:

	Total
t 422; *d* 334	756
n 429; *m* 183	612
r 384; *l* 205	589
s 282; *z* 189	471
th 276; *dh* 39	315
f 106; *v* 146	252
p 135; *b* 97	232
k 125; *g* 39	164
ch 49; *j* 34	83
sh 40; *zh* 7	47

Lineality: According to Mr. Pitman, the horizontal letters in our system—*n, m, r, l, k, g*—total 1,365.

Balance: The downward characters—*s, z, f, v, p, b, ch, j, sh, zh*—total 1,085. The upward characters—*t, d, th*—total 1,071.

It will be seen that, according to Mr. Pitman's figures, there is an almost perfect balance between the upward and downward characters in our system. It will also be seen that there is a much higher percentage of lineal movement than either upward or downward movement.

THE APPLICATION OF MR. CROSS'S FIGURES.   Mr. Cross's values, when the letters are paired, are as follows:

	Total
n 163; *m* 67	230
r 144; *l* 76	220
t 137; *d* 80	217
s 85; *z* 81	166
p 40; *b* 53	93
th 80	80
k 52; *g* 22	74
f 36; *v* 37	73
sh 11; *zh* 3; *ch* 16; *j* 18	48

Lineality: Based on this table, the horizontal characters in our system—*n, m, r, l, k, g*—total 542.

Balance: The downward characters—*s, z, p, b, f, v, sh, zh, ch, j*—total 380; the upward characters—*t, d, th*—total 297.

From Mr. Cross's figures it will also be seen that there is a very close balance in our system between upward and downward characters —especially when the minute character of *s* and *z* is considered. It will also be seen that once more the horizontal characters almost equal the *combined total of upward and downward characters.* Bear in mind, too, what was said about the onward nature of *t* and *d*. In Mr. Cross's table, too, the letter *t*, which is expressed by a very short upward character in our system, is given almost double the value of *d*.

Natural movement: Still another factor, and one of equal importance, is the use made of the movement that is most frequent in longhand—the movement embodied in the small longhand forms of the vowels, *a, e, i, o, u,* and in the small forms of nearly all the consonants. It will be seen that *r, l, p, b,* which are written with that motion in our system, have a total of 313, while *k, g, f, v,* characters with the opposite movement, which is much less frequent in longhand, have a total of less than one-half that number—147. I shall have occasion to refer to some of these factors in explaining the construction of the alphabet.

Since writing the foregoing I came across another table prepared by Sir Edward Clarke, K. C. In the Preface to his system, "Easy Shorthand," Sir Edward says:

> The result obtained from a careful examination of a large number of passages from different books is that the twelve symbols we require to use most often are those representing the following consonants, in their order of frequency: *s, n, t, r, d, f, l, m, p, b, g, k.*

The table is not complete and is given merely as a matter of record.

THE FREQUENCY OF THE VOWELS. While I have given tables compiled by several authors about the comparative values of the various consonants, I am unable to do so with regard to the vowels. The reason for this is the scant consideration given to the vowels in the older systems. There was no need to give much attention to the frequency-value of the vowels in the construction of systems in which vowels were expressed, if expressed at all, by dots or by dots and dashes, since they were all on an equality in the physical effort of executing them.

I am, therefore, especially sorry that the tables I had compiled were lost in the fire which destroyed my offices in 1900. The figures about the frequency of the various vowels would be of great interest and importance in dealing with the allocation of the signs for the vowels. Fortunately, I remember, in a general way at least, the results of my investigations of the occurrences of the vowels more vividly than those of the consonants, because they were responsible for the radical change which I made in the manner of using the circles and hooks for the expression of the vowel sounds.

I found that *i* (as in *it*) was by far the most frequent sound in the language. As I remember it, the figures showed that this sound occurred almost twice as often as any other vowel sound and occurred as frequently as *all* the vowel sounds of *a* combined! Next in importance to short *i* were short *e* and the short *a*, with very little difference in value; next came the long *e* and the long *a*, and here again there was little difference. The sound of *a*, as in *arm*, was not very common. Next to these came the short *o* as in *hot*, and the long *o* as in *no*, with little difference in value between them. The sound of *aw* was much less frequent. The sound of *u* as in *up* was almost as frequent as *o*, but short *oo* and long *oo* were low in the scale.

Briefly stated: when grouped, the three vowels, short *i*, short *e*, and long *e*, had fully twice the value of the three sounds of *a;* the three sounds of *a* were at least one-third more frequent than the *o* vowels; the *o* vowels were about one-third more frequent than the short *u*, short *oo*, and long *oo*.

Although about thirty-five years have passed since I compiled these figures, I believe that any scientific investigation of the frequency of occurrence of the vowel sounds will show that my recollection of them is very close to the actual values.

The question remains—if the vowels *are* to be written in the outline, how shall they be represented?

I believe that many authors of joined-vowel systems have failed to achieve their object because they did not reach a sound judgment on this point. Through long practice of disjoined-vowel shorthand, many authors have attempted to retain certain facile characters for the representation of frequent consonants and were then forced to adopt less facile material for the expression of the vowels—with disastrous results. It seems to me to be very obvious that if the vowels *are* to be written in the outline the most facile of all shorthand signs should be used for their expression. The frequency and the very nature of vowels render that imperative.

As Mr. D. Kimball put it:

> Consonants are to a word what the bones are to the body—the large, strong framework. Vowels are to words what the flesh is to the body: they give to them form, flexibility, volume. It is desirable that the two classes of sounds should be represented by letters readily distinguishable. To the consonants should be assigned large letters, and it is best that the vowels should be represented by small letters.

Application of the Basic Principles in the Representation of Consonants

> *A compound character should never be used in a system until all the simple lines of nature are exhausted.*
>
> HISTORY OF SHORTHAND.—James H. Lewis

> *Related letters should have related signs, which may be differentiated by length or thickness; the single consonant character should consist of a single stroke or curve.*
>
> —Edward Pocknell

> *As a general rule,* sounds *within a determined degree of likeness should be represented by* signs *within a determined degree of likeness.*
>
> —Edwin Guest

Three of the seven basic principles discussed in previous chapters do not call for further comment in explaining the construction of the alphabet. These three principles are: the longhand slope of the characters, the elimination of shading, and the elimination of position writing. If these are accepted as fundamental principles, they are not affected by the selection or allocation of the characters; nor is the selection or allocation of the characters affected by them except that they exclude from consideration shaded characters, vertical characters, and backslope characters.

The other four basic principles require discussion because they are susceptible to varying methods of treatment. As it is possible to express joined vowels in many different ways, it is necessary to discuss the method in which their expression in our system differs from that of other joined-vowel systems. Obviously, too, as the allocation of the characters to the letters in the alphabet will determine the degree of lineality, of curvilinear motion, and the frequency of obtuse angles, in the writing, these features require discussion.

THE GOVERNING FACTORS. Anyone who has given the alphabet of the system and the combinations of the alphabet any thought will have realized that there were three factors which governed the selection of characters to represent the consonants. Those three factors were: (1) curvilinear motion, as expressed in the oval; (2) the elimination of the obtuse angle through the blending principle; (3) lineality. With the first two of these I was entering upon untrodden fields, since they were absolutely new theories in shorthand construction—and yet they were simple, natural, logical.

The formulation of these two principles was the culmination of a long series of more or less empirical efforts at system construction. I believed that these principles were extremely important discoveries— so important that I determined to test both of them with *every possible combination of letters* before making the allocation of the characters.

THE ELLIPSE ANALYZED.   It seems to me that the best way to begin an exposition of the construction of the alphabet is to go back to the foundation. As explained in the first article of this series, the system is based, primarily, on the elements of longhand writing; and the basis of longhand writing is the oval or ellipse. The first thing to do, then, is to analyze the ellipse.

It is very easy to ascertain the elements of the ellipse. If you write the ordinary longhand letter *o,* and dissect it, you will see that it is composed of five elements—the downward curve, the turn at the bottom, the upward curve, the small circle or oval, and the connecting stroke.

Now write the entire alphabet in the small letters of longhand, and count the letters in which that lower turn (which expresses *r* in our system) is to be found. You will find that the lower turn occurs in no less than *nineteen* of the twenty-six letters of the alphabet. The exceptions are *h, j, m, n, p, s,* and *z;* and you will notice that the *connecting stroke after four of these letters is made with the lower turn.* It is important to note that every vowel-sign in longhand contains that lower turn; and in one of them (*u*) it occurs twice. Furthermore, the connecting stroke *after every vowel* contains it.

Carry the inquiry a little farther, and you will notice that the first two elements of the oval or ellipse (see illustration No. 1) occur *in combination* in nearly every letter of the alphabet.

I do not think that I need to point out the importance of the facts disclosed by this analysis. In themselves they furnish an acid test that may be applied to any system founded on the longhand-movement basis. (It is well, however, to keep in mind two points mentioned in a previous article: the importance of the *combination,* and the importance of the *phonetic pairs* of letters.)

That I was blind to this important truth at the time of one of my earlier efforts at shorthand construction ("Script Phonography") is shown by the fact that I allocated that most facile character, the lower turn, to the representation of *k*—one of the least frequent consonants in the language—and on a smaller scale (as a hook), to the least-frequent group of vowels.

Reverting for a moment to the analysis of the longhand alphabet: it is important to keep in mind that the *upward* turn occurs only in *h, m, n, p, z.* The use made of this less-valuable element in assigning characters to the consonants and vowels will be explained later. The predominance of the other motion, on account of its being used in all but seven consonants, and in *all* the vowels, explains why most people, when they attempt to write rapidly in longhand, have difficulty in distinguishing *n* from *u;* and why the forms of other letters, such as *m, p,* which contain the upward turn, show the same tendency. Speaking of this tendency, in his address as President of the Shorthand Society, London, Mr. Theodore R. Wright said: "That this curve is one of the easiest to form is proved by the well-known fact that in rapid writing *u*'s and *n*'s are very commonly made alike. On examination, however, I believe it will invariably be found that this arises from the *n* being made like *u,* never from *u* being made like *n.*"

In a series of lessons entitled "Commercial Penmanship: How to Acquire a Free and Fluent Style" (*Pitman's Journal,* March 30, 1918), Mr. G. C. Jarvis, B. A., said:

> Of all the twenty-six letters of the alphabet small *e* and small *i* are the simplest in outline and the quickest made. . . . Words like *mamma, mawk,* and *now* take much longer to write than words like *level, eels,* and *lee.*

This quotation emphasizes in a striking way the points I have been trying to explain.

THE SELECTION AND ALLOCATION OF MATERIAL—R AND L. The reason why I assigned the facile downward curve to the very frequent letters, *r* and *l,* is now fairly obvious. As shown by the tables given in the preceding article, *r* is one of three most frequent letters in the language; and while *l* is not so frequent, the pairing of these letters gives great frequency to the character (short and long) used to express them. The liquids *r* and *l* coalesce with other letters to form "consonantal diphthongs," as they have been termed—*pr, pl, br, bl, fr, fl, kr, kl, gr, gl,* etc.—and this has been so well recognized that in many systems purely arbitrary, and sometimes very illogical, methods of expression have been adopted for such combinations. In Pitman's Shorthand, for example, in writing the simple word *apple,* a hook for *l* is written, then the *p,* and finally the dot for the vowel, so that the exact order in which the letters for *apple* are written is *l-p-a!* Isaac Pitman & Sons, *Handbook for Shorthand Teachers,* has this candid statement: "Another difficulty with regard to initial hooks is that of making the pupils understand that the *r* and *l* are to be read AFTER and not before the consonant to which the hook is attached. The tendency among beginners is to read them in the wrong order."

It follows from what we have said that the lower turn, which occurs in nearly all the letters of longhand, joins easily with characters founded on longhand, if the characters have been selected with that end in view, and the allocation of that lower turn to *r* and *l* is, therefore, both logical and eminently practical.

The pairing of the liquids is logical, natural, and very practical. They are paired in two of the most successful of modern systems— Duployé and Stolze, in *Eclectic Shorthand* by J. George Cross, in *Edeography* by F. Redfern, in *Lucid Shorthand* by William George Spencer (father of the great English philosopher and scientist, Herbert Spencer), in *British Phonography* by Edward J. Jones—as well as many others. Mr. Hugh B. Innes, LL. B., in *The Office* (London, June 15, 1889), said:

> In Stolze *l* and *r* are circles of different sizes, while in my own acquaintance with Gurney, I find that *r* and *l* written carelessly are remarkably alike, and that coalescing r may be, and in the examples of the published handbook often is, omitted without causing any trouble. In Taylor, the two letters are clearly distinguished by a loop, but in hurried Phonography the upward *l* and *r* bear a striking resemblance to one another and the two sizes of hooks by which these letters are affixed to a group are not easily distinguished.

The point mentioned by Mr. Innes about *r* and *l* being paired in Isaac Pitman Shorthand in the case of the small and large hooks before curves is ignored by Pitman advocates, just as is the fact that in practical writing *s* and *z* are expressed by the same sign—a circle; and that *sh* and *zh* are expressed alike in a great many words.

Some of the pairings in Pitmanic shorthand are absolutely indefensible. In Isaac Pitman, Benn Pitman, and Graham, *mp* is paired with *m;* in Isaac Pitman's early editions, and in Benn Pitman, Graham, and other Pitmanic "styles," the downward *l* is paired with *y* and downward *r* with *w;* while Munson pairs *m* with *h!* Mr. D. L. Scott-Browne, editor of *Browne's Phonographic Monthly,* said:

> "Mr. Munson insists that the sign for *h* employed by Benn Pitman, Graham, etc., and that used for the same purpose by Isaac Pitman, is unphilosophical because they introduce *compound* signs where harmony requires a simple one; and so far as that is concerned, he is right."

P AND B. Starting with the combination idea, and basing that idea on the elements of the ellipse or oval, it did not require any great amount of thought to decide upon the allocation of the downward left curve to *p* and *b,* since that curve precedes the lower turn in *a, e, o,* etc., in longhand, thus providing the constantly recurring *pr, pl, br, bl,* with

easy, natural, graceful combinations. So easy is that movement that it requires very little more effort to make any of these combinations than it does to make the lower turn alone. If you will look at a page of the writing in the system, you will be impressed with the grace and beauty which these combinations give to the writing.

In view of the natural, effortless character of the combination used for *pr,* etc., it is simply amazing how little use has been made of it in the older systems. Consider what it represents in other well-known systems: in Pitmanic shorthand it expresses *ln* (and only one of the forms for *ln*), as in *alone* and one or two other infrequent words; in Duployé, and in the numerous adaptations of Duployé to English by Pernin, Sloan, Brandt, Perrault, and others, it expresses *w-s*—two letters which do not combine without an intervening vowel; in Script Phonography it represents *ch-k* or *j-k,* which do not combine without an intervening vowel. Similar illustrations could be given from other systems.

K AND G. The upward turn, found in the longhand signs for *m, n, p, h, z,* being much less frequent than the downward curve, was assigned to *k, g,* because these letters are much less frequent than *r* or *l.* In making this allocation, I had in mind the fact that in a large percentage of the cases where *k* or *g* do occur, they are in conjunction with either *r* or *l,* as *kr (cr), kl (cl), gr, gl,* and by this allocation these combinations are expressed by easy curve combinations.

F AND V. The letters *f* and *v* are not frequent; hence, the less useful right curve, which occurs in the longhand *v* and *z* is used for them. By the allocation made to *f* and *v* one of the most graceful combinations in the system—*fr, fl, vr, vl*—was obtained, a combination that occurs in writing *v* and other letters in longhand. The selection of the characters for *f, v* was influenced to some extent by the possibility of securing the "egg-shaped" blends which are used for *def, dev, tive.*

In a preceding paragraph I mentioned the failure of authors of older systems to appreciate the value of the simple, natural combination used in our system for *pr, br,* etc. It seems to me to be equally remarkable that the combination used in our system for *fr* was not used for *any purpose* in any of the many hundreds of systems that have appeared since shorthand history began. It is not, perhaps, surprising that the angle was not eliminated in geometric systems, but it is surprising that systems on the longhand basis did not blend these characters, as is done in our system. Probably the reason is to be found in the fact that in previous systems the curve used in our system for *f, v* was assigned to letters which do not combine in speech with those expressed by the horizontal downward curve.

SH, CH, J. The straight, downward line is easy to write *independently;* but, as Mr. Callendar said, it is rigid and inelastic when joined to other characters, hence its assignment to *sh, ch, j,* which are not frequently occurring sounds.

I have always thought that I was particularly fortunate in the grouping of *sh, ch, j.* It is well known that it is much easier to control the length of downward straight lines than it is to control onward lines. The distinction between *sh, ch,* and *j* can be maintained very easily— the tick for *sh* being a mere drop of the pen, such as is used in the first part of the bookkeeper's check mark. The beauty of it is that even when the distinction is *not* observed there is no trouble in reading the forms correctly. If *French* becomes *Frensh,* or even *frenj,* it does not matter in the least. Hundreds of other illustrations are already familiar to you.

The expression of *sh* and *zh* and *ch* and *j* by entirely different characters (although the sounds are closely related) has created one of the most troublesome of the many problems with which Pitmanic authors have had to deal. To show how serious this problem has been, I quote the following from Benn Pitman's "Life and Labors of Sir Isaac Pitman":

> Phoneticians have abundant reason for thinking that after fifty years of investigation and discussion, pioneered by Sir Isaac Pitman, they have settled a great many perplexing questions of use, practice, and application; nevertheless, there are opinions still held by intelligent persons which, from their standpoints, may be regarded as yet unsettled.
>
> For example, do we use *ch* or *sh* as the terminal sound in the words *French, bunch, pinch, filch,* etc.? It is amusing to find so great a stickler for the right thing as Isaac Pitman—and "right" with him had a moral side to it, and meant more than "correct,"—giving *sh* in his Phonographic Dictionary for 1846, *ch* in the edition of 1850, *sh* in the edition of 1852, *sh* in the edition of 1867, and *ch* in the 1878 and subsequent editions, as the correct pronunciation of this class of words. But with seeming inconsistency, *sh* continued to be used in a few words, as *filch, Welch,* in editions of his dictionary, as late as 1883, 1891, and 1893. H. T. Jansen (Exeter, England), one of our early patrons and phonetic enthusiasts, whose opinion Isaac Pitman ranked with that of Dr. Ellis, Dr. William Gregory, Sir Walter Trevelyan, and a few others of his earlier advisers, insisted that it was "simply absurd" to write this class of words with other than *sh* as the terminal sound. Dr. Gregory (Edinburgh) characterized the use of *ch* in these words as "the greatest absurdity possible."

It seems to me that there could not be a stronger endorsement of the method of expressing *sh* and *ch* by the same character, differing slightly in length, than is contained in this quotation from Benn Pitman; nor could there be a more convincing argument against *expressing them by entirely different characters.* Just consider the perplexity of the ordinary student when Isaac Pitman, after many years of close study of phonetics, and with the assistance of the greatest authorities on the subject, could not tell definitely whether a word should be written with *sh* or *ch*—sounds which are represented in his system by *entirely different characters.*

In our system the student is relieved of that problem. My observation is that in such words the student of our system follows the ordinary spelling instinctively and makes the characters *ch* length. Anyway, he is never bothered about it one way or another.

There are other reasons why the allocation of the straight oblique stroke to *sh, ch, j,* seems to me to have been extremely felicitous. As *sh* expresses *shun,* that very common termination is disposed of by a facile downward tick that joins easily *after* all characters. If you have studied Pitman's Shorthand, you will probably remember the numerous rules (and exceptions to rules) governing the use of the large *shun hook.* Pitman's "Centenary Instructor" contains several pages devoted to *shun,* and Taylor's "Commentary on Pitman's Shorthand" devotes no less than *fifteen pages in small type* to that momentous subject! In our system it is disposed of in four words: "Write *sh* for *shun.*"

Again if a careless writer occasionally writes *s* without curving it, the *s may* resemble *sh.* In that event, *s-k-e-m* (scheme) will be read as *sh-k-e-m,* disguise as *dish-guise*—and there can be no misreading. Of course, the inclusion of the vowels in the outline is largely responsible for the legibility of the forms in such cases.

The combinations *sht, shd, cht, chd, jt, jd,* are very frequent at the end of words; thus *lashed, reached, matched, preached, beached, wished, lodged,* and they are all easily expressed. These are extremely facile combinations in themselves, but they also preserve *balance* between the upward and downward characters by bringing the hand back to the line of writing. Take the word *alleged,* for instance: the downward stroke *j* is followed by the upward stroke *d,* which brings the hand back to the line without an "ineffectual movement of the pen." If you write in our system, "It is alleged that he preached," you will see the great advantage derived from this arrangement of these characters.

s AND z. The expression of *s* was one of the greatest of my problems in the construction of the alphabet. The letter *s* is an exceedingly common letter, and it is constantly used in conjunction with every other letter. Above all other letters, therefore, *s* demanded flexibility. In consonance with the curvilinear theory, it ought to be represented by a *curve;* but a *full-size* curve for such a common letter would militate against compactness and facility in many words.

My experience with three adaptations of Duployé had impressed me with the mobility of the little "quadrants" used in Duployé for the ever-recurring nasal sounds of French, *an, en, in, on, un.* These signs are not very useful in English for the purpose to which they are applied in French (which is one of the weak points in adaptations of the French system to English), but their selection for the expression of the all-important nasal sounds of French made a deep impression on me. I do not suppose I should have paid much attention to them if I had known only the Pernin or Sloan adaptations of Duployé. It was when I mastered the adaptation by J. P. A. Martin, which adhered very closely to the plan of using the quadrants as in the original Duployé, that the value of these signs became apparent to me.

So little did I value them in my earlier efforts at shorthand construction that I assigned no less than four of them (written downward in all directions) to the almost useless *h!* What was still worse, I assigned two of them (written upward) to *n.* That was primitive, indeed, because it apparently ranked *h* as of greater importance than *n!* Even if only *two* downward quadrants had been assigned to *h,* it would have ranked the aspirate higher than *n,* because the downward quadrants are more easily made than those written upward. A little experimentation will show that in writing upward characters, particularly curves, the pen is held more rigidly than in writing downward characters. The downward curves are written with much greater flexibility, and usually with much greater curvature, than upward curves. The downward quadrants are not only more flexible but they join easily with other characters, while the small upward quadrants join awkwardly to many characters, except at the beginning and end of words, and should, therefore, be used for the representation of comparatively infrequent letters.

(Incidentally, the word "quadrant" is an incorrect word to use in speaking of these small curves in our system. A "quadrant" is a "quarter circle," and while it is a correct description of these small curves in the Duployan and other *geometric* systems founded on the circle and its segments, the small curves used for *s* and *th* in our system are not "quarter circles," but halves of small *ellipses*.)

The facile, flexible little curves were assigned to *s* and *z;* and naturally the downward curves were given the preference. How admirably these little curves join to other characters, and with what little pen effort, is known to every writer of the system.

At this point it may be well to point out that the insertion of the vowels has a great bearing on the value of these signs. Sometimes a writer of another system, in giving our system a hasty examination, jumps to the conclusion that *s* will clash with *p* or with *f* in rapid writing when the distinction of size is not observed. Sometimes they would—if it were not for the joined vowels. What I mean is that if *s* is written *very carelessly*—both as to *size* and *shape*—so that *sp* appears as *pp*, it does not make any material difference. Why? Because the reader knows that *pp* cannot occur without an intervening *vowel*. The outline could not be read *peep, pap, pop, Pope, pup, poop, pipe,* simply because the vowel would be written in each of these words. For the same reason *sf* could not be *ff*—and so on with all the other combinations.

There is another difference: since *s* is a very minute character, there is a rule that the downward consonant *following s* rests on the line; therefore, if the *s* is made as large as *p* in writing *sp,* the fact that the *second* character rests on the line shows that it is *sp,* not *pp.* The writer does that automatically.

In addition to all this, as writers of the system know, there is a distinctiveness about the deep curvature of the minute form for *s* in practical writing that is quite remarkable.

I have previously spoken of the analogy of both *sound* and *sign* existing between *s* and *sh*—a scientific point worth noting, in connection with the representation of *s.*

TH.   The less facile little upward curve was assigned to *th;* and its analogy, both in *sign* and *sound,* to *t* is already clear to you.

At the period of my earlier experiments I was largely influenced by my enthusiasm for Duployé, and therefore inclined to undervalue *th.* As this sound does not occur in French, there was, of course, no provision for it in the original Duployé. All the adaptations of Duployé to English (except that of Brandt, with which I was not then acquainted) expressed *th* by the sign for *t* with a dot over it.

In practice the dot was dropped, and such words as *debt* and *death, bat* and *bath, tin* and *thin, tea* and *thee, toes* and *those, tick* and *thick,* were expressed by the same outlines. Yet full provision was made for *sh* because that sound is important in French, while *j* was neglected in nearly all the adaptations!

In one of my earlier efforts at system construction I perpetrated even a greater crime against phonetics than this. As already mentioned, I assigned no less than four little downward curves to the aspirate, which was certainly a generous provision for such an unimportant element, especially in a system in which the vowels were expressed in the outlines. That was bad enough; but I went a step farther and expressed *th* by joining *t* to *h!* When *th* was written in full in this way most of the outlines containing it were simply atrocious; and it was necessary to omit *h,* as was done in the Duployan adaptations. This was worse than the plan adopted by most of the Duployan adaptations, bad as that was, because in these adaptations the omission of the *dot* did not change the *form of the word;* but after a student had acquired the habit of joining two *strokes* for *th,* it was difficult for him to drop one of them. When he did drop it, *the form of the word underwent a radical change.* Every experienced writer and teacher will understand what that meant!

In a joined-vowel system the expression of *h* at the beginning of a word, where *h* usually occurs, is unimportant. If *happy* becomes *'appy*—or *hope* becomes *'ope*—there can be no possible misreading; but its omission in *th,* a sound which may occur in any part of a word, is a very serious matter, as will be seen from the illustrations already given.

In breaking away from the Duployan plan of slighting *th,* I was probably influenced by my previous knowledge of other systems; but I think that what impressed me with the absurdity of expressing the *single sound* of *th* by *two* characters, or expressing it in practice by *t,* was the criticism of that expedient by all writers of Phonography. It was manifestly a violation of *phonetics,* which no argument could overcome.

The reasons which governed the assignment of the characters to express *r, l, p, b, f, v, k, g, sh, ch, j, s,* and *th* have now been given. I have purposely reserved *n* and *m, t,* and *d* for the last.

N AND M. In explaining the process of reasoning which led to the discovery of the blending principle, I said that the principle was tested on every possible combination of letters. These tests demonstrated conclusively that by far the best results were obtained by assigning the horizontal lines to *n* and *m,* and the upward lines to *t* and *d.* This allocation yielded the beautiful and facile blends for *ten, den, tem, dem, ent, end, emt, emd*—and eliminated obtuse angles, which have been execrated by shorthand writers since the beginning of shorthand history. It also promoted curvilinear motion to a remarkable extent.

By the way, if you go back to the longhand illustrations of the vowels and consonants, you will notice that the curve used for *ent, end,* is the *finishing* curve of the oval, and of nearly every letter in long-hand. It is peculiarly fitting, therefore, that it should express *ent, end, mt, md,* which are generally terminal.

The relationship of sound between *n* and *m* is very close; they are also of similar appearance in longhand, and are, therefore, very easily mastered and associated mentally. Speaking of these letters, Isaac Pitman in his address on "The Science of Shorthand" (Shorthand Society, London, 1884) said:

> *M* and *n* are not only side by side in the alphabet, but like loving sisters, they walk through the language hand in hand. These affinities must be regarded in the selection of signs to represent the sounds, so that the letters may run easily into each other as the sounds do.

It will be recognized that the dictum of the author of "Phonography" applies more strongly to the representation of *n* and *m* in Gregg Shorthand than it does to his own system. In our system *n* is expressed by a short horizontal stroke and *m* by a long horizontal stroke, corresponding to the difference in their size in longhand and to the *length of the sounds of these letters.* The tables given in the previous chapter show that *n* has more than double the frequency value of *m;* therefore *n* should be expressed by a short sign and *m* by a long one.

Application of the Basic Principles in the Representation of Vowels

THE joining of the characters for the sounds, consonants and vowels, as they occur in the word is so natural and logical that there is only one possible reason for disjoining the vowels, which is that the insertion of the vowels would lengthen the forms unduly. That was a valid objection to the earlier systems containing joined vowels, and also to some of the more recent systems in which the vowels were represented by strokes; but, as I have shown in previous chapters, that objection was eliminated by the use of more facile material, and a more scientific use of that material.

The speed and accuracy records made by young writers of Gregg Shorthand in the national shorthand speed contests—records that have never been equaled by writers of any disjoined-vowel systems, or, in fact, of any other system, have demonstrated decisively that joined-vowels do not necessarily entail a loss of speed.

The origin and development of the use of the circles and hooks as the logical material for the expression of the vowels was traced in some of the earlier chapters. This method of expressing vowels originated with the early English shorthand authors, but in France—through Conen de Prépéan, Aimé-Paris, and Duployé—the principle gradually evolved into a more and more perfect adaptation to the needs of the French language.

The use of diacritical marks to distinguish slight differences of sound probably suggested itself to French shorthand authors because diacritical marks are used so much in French to indicate the accent of vowels, and in the French shorthand systems diacritical marks are used to indicate differences in the nasal sounds, *an, en, in, on, un,* as well as the vowels.

In the adaptations of the French systems to English the diacritical marks were used without any scientific classification of the vowels. In the Sloan-Duployan, a dot was used above a vowel to mark a short sound; a dot below to mark a medium sound and sometimes a long sound; and a horizontal dash was also used. It was a haphazard arrangement.

THE ORIGIN OF THE VOWEL GROUPS. In the "Story of Gregg Shorthand" I referred to the fine accomplishments in school of my brother George and my sister Fanny, the latter having taken first prize every year in the girls' school she attended, and George having secured first place every year with the exception of one year when he won second place. George died in New Zealand of tuberculosis at the early age of twenty-four, and Fanny died in Glasgow two years later. Fanny was the only one of the family who displayed any conspicuous ability as a speaker or musician, and it was through her study of elocution and singing that she became a member of the faculty of the Glasgow Institution for the Deaf and Dumb. I believe it was owing to the extraordinary zeal and enthusiasm with which she devoted herself to the great and beneficent calling that she so exhausted her strength that she passed away when but twenty-eight years of age. I had then, and have now, a profound reverence for her abilities, and a still more profound reverence for her many lovable qualities both of heart and mind.

Kindly in nature as they were, my three brothers looked upon my enthusiasm for shorthand as a species of mania. That I had the audacity to dream of attempting the construction of a new system, even if for my own use only, seemed to them the quintessence of folly, and it afforded them endless opportunities for merriment at my expense. At such times it was to Fanny that I went for consolation. While not in the least interested in shorthand, she was always sympathetic and encouraging. Looking backward, I can now understand that, as a true teacher, she knew that *any* subject in which I became really interested, and to which I devoted continuous attention, would be likely to aid my mental development.

One of the problems I discussed with her was the classification of the vowels. That was a subject on which she could speak with authority, by virtue of her studies and her daily work in teaching the deaf and dumb. At that time I was putting the finishing touches on "Script Phonography," in which I had adopted for the most part the Duployan arrangement of the vowels and also to a large extent the unsystematic arrangement of them in the leading adaptation of Duployé.

On account of my previous experience with the grouping or pairing of the vowels in Pitman's Shorthand, I was dissatisfied with the unsystematic manner of distinguishing the shades of sound by dots above, dots below, and horizontal dashes, and dots inside circles and loops employed in Sloan-Duployan. Fanny patiently explained the relationship of the various vowel-sounds, showed me some books which she had on the subject, and suggested the *grouping* which I incorporated in the system on which I was then working, and which I retained in Light-Line.

I shall devote a few paragraphs to an explanation of this plan of grouping the vowels. To quote from the Gregg Shorthand Manual, "In writing by sound, there are twelve distinct vowels, which are arranged in four groups, each group consisting of three closely related sounds."

Now as to the method of grouping the vowels:

GROUP ONE.   The first group consists of ă, ä, ā, as in *at, art, ate.* Since these three sounds of *a,* as well as others, are written and printed with exactly the same character in the English language without confusion, and in Gregg Shorthand the number of sounds of *a* represented by one character is restricted to three, it is even more exact than longhand. The grouping of these three sounds of *a* not only simplifies the learning of the system, but simplifies the reading of it.

Even authorities on phonetics are often puzzled over the exact sound of *a* in *senate, palace, bondage, desolate,* and thousands of other words; and it will be obvious that the expression of these sounds by the same character in practice relieves the student of a very puzzling element in the study of shorthand. The language itself is fluid and flexible—particularly in the vocal sounds—and there is a decided advantage in relieving the shorthand student of phonetic problems of this kind.

GROUP TWO.   The second group consists of *ĭ, ĕ, ē,* as in *pit, pet, peat.* This is a logical grouping. In his "Art of Phonography" Mr. Munson devotes a long paragraph to showing the close relationship between *i* and *e.* He says:

> The sound of *ĕ* in *term,* and its precise equivalent, the sound of *ĭ* in *mirth,* are provided with two signs, the light dot and the light dash in the second place, it being optional with the writer which shall be used.

The relationship of *ĕ* and *ē* is also commented upon by Mr. Munson, and he gives a long list of words to illustrate this relationship —*elude, economy, elastic, becalm, below, demean, secure, acme, eolian,* as well as some words in which *i* is used in ordinary writing, such as *finance, divide, pacify.* It seems to me that a close study of these words will be sufficient to show how logical is the grouping of the sounds in our system. As has been frequently pointed out by phoneticians and lexicographers, there is a tendency to shorten *e* in many words where formerly it was given the long sound, *e.g.,* in *been, becalm, below,* and other words beginning with *be.*

The expression of both these closely related sounds in our system not only relieves the student of a very puzzling element in the study of shorthand, but establishes uniformity in the shorthand forms used in all parts of the English-speaking world.

GROUP THREE.   This group consists of *ŏ, ö, ō,* as in *hot, orb, oar.* This is a very natural grouping and a very suggestive one, both in the writing of shorthand and in the reading of it. It eliminates hesitancy in writing words about which there may be a doubt as to the exact vowel sound, as *economy, oblivion*—and many other words.

GROUP FOUR.   This group consists of *ŭ, ŏŏ, ōō.* The close relationship here will be seen by pronouncing *tuck, took, tomb.* It is so logical and natural that I do not need to discuss it.

I may add, incidentally, that the simplicity of our vowel grouping is one of the secrets of the remarkable success of the system in the writing of foreign languages—notably Spanish, for which language it has been adopted exclusively by the United States Government in the high schools of Puerto Rico.

A point that is not understood by writers of disjoined-vowel systems is this: that in most words there can be but one possible vowel. For example, *l-a-t,* as *late,* because there is no such word as *lat; k-i-t,* as *kit,* because there are no such words as *ket* or *keet*—and so on *ad infinitum.* After the student has written the forms for *late, kit,* etc., two or three times, he recognizes them at *sight*—no analysis is needed. And even when the form expresses two words, as *led* and *lead,* the context in nearly every instance tells explicitly what the word is, as: "He *led* the way," or, "He will *lead* the way." (It will be noted that in this instance, as in many others, *the same form for both sounds is used in longhand,* as in the sentences: "He will *lead* the way." "Let me have a *lead* pencil." "He is working in a *lead* mine.")

MATERIAL USED SCIENTIFICALLY. Much more important than the grouping of the vowels was the radical change which I made in the manner of using the material—circles and hooks—for the expression of the vowels or vowel-groups.

In the French systems of Duployé, Aimé-Paris, and others, the small circle expresses *a* and the large circle, *o;* and other vowels were expressed by hooks in various directions. That plan was followed in the various adaptations of the French systems to English; and it was the one adopted in my early experiments. The investigation of the frequency of the various sounds revealed the fact that this allocation was utterly unscientific because "the figures showed that short *i* occurred twice as often as any other vowel sound and occurred as frequently as all the vowel sounds of *a* combined; and that if the short *e* and the long *e* were grouped with the short *i,* the frequency-value of the sign expressing the group was vastly greater than that of any other vowel or group of vowels."

Therefore, the logical manner of expressing that particular group (*ĭ, ĕ, ē*) was to assign to it the most facile sign, the small circle. The *a* group came next in frequency, and therefore the logical representation of that group was the next most facile sign—the large circle.

There remained the expression of the *ŏ, aw, ō* group, and the *ŭ, ŏŏ, ōō* group. Here again a radical change from former practice was necessary. Based on the analysis of the oval or ellipse, given in a previous chapter, it was easy to see that since *ŏ, aw, ō* occurred more frequently than *ŭ, ŏŏ, ōō,* the familiar downward turn, in the form of a small hook, should express the former group, and the less frequent upward turn should express the latter group.

I could spend a good deal of time explaining the enormous advantages derived from this departure from the old methods of using circles and hooks, but I believe it is unnecessary to do so.

THE FOUR DISTINCTIVE FEATURES. There are four important differences between our system and other joined-vowel systems in which the circles and hooks are used for the expression of the vowels:

First. The circles and hooks are assigned to the vowels in Gregg Shorthand in accordance with the frequency-value of the sounds and the facility-value of the material. In the old phrase, "the most facile characters are assigned to the most frequently occurring sounds." This was not the case with any previous system.

Second. There is uniformity in the method of marking the distinctions between the shades of sound, the marks being always placed *beneath* the vowel instead of *above* and *below*. There is a decided gain through the uniformity of practice. This was not done in any previous system.

Third. The use of the *acute accent mark* to indicate the *long* sound of the vowel—a very natural and suggestive plan which was not used by any system prior to the publication of "Light-Line Phonography."

Fourth. The vowels are classified scientifically in accordance with the nature of the sounds. The *Lingual Vowels* (ă, ä, ā, ĭ, ĕ, ē), so called because they are formed mainly by the modulation of the tongue, are expressed by *circles;* the *Labial Vowels* (ŏ, aw, ō, ŭ, ŏŏ, ōō,), so called because they are formed mainly by the modulation of the lips, are expressed by *hooks*. This scientific division of the two classes of vowel sounds had not been made in any joined-vowel system prior to "Light-Line Phonography."

The Evolution of Shorthand Principles

> *The whole drift of modern science and art is towards naturalness. To copy the simplicity of Nature is found to be the highest wisdom.*
> —David P. Lindsley

Seeing that the value of each of the principles discussed in this book has been so generally acknowledged by authors and advocates of nearly all systems of shorthand, as shown by the quotations from their writings, the question naturally suggests itself: Why have not these principles been generally adopted in the construction of shorthand systems?

The answer is to be found in the conservatism with which mankind approaches a new thought or a new invention.

Incidentally, we may add that this applies to shorthand more than to most subjects, because shorthand involves physical expression of the thought. After a time the physical response to the mental impulse becomes subconscious and automatic, like walking, and it is exceedingly difficult to think in forms, or to use forms, other than those with which the mind and hand have become familiar by "long use and wont."

This explains why it is that every system of shorthand that has attained distinction in any language or country, by reason of its *originality,* has been the product of youth. The most popular of the German systems, that of Gabelsberger, was originated when its author was twenty-seven; the most popular of the French systems, that of Émile Duployé, was produced when its author was twenty-six; the most popular system in England, that of Isaac Pitman, was published when its author was twenty-four; and the most popular system in America was published when its author was twenty.

ORIGIN OF GEOMETRIC STYLES. Quite recently—and since the preceding chapters of this book were written—I had occasion to make some investigations of the Tironian notes, which were in use before the birth of Christ, and also of the English systems of the sixteenth and seventeenth centuries, for the purpose of preparing a brief history of shorthand. In the course of these investigations I became convinced that the authors of the earliest English systems were not only inspired to attempt the revival of the art by reading Plutarch's statement that the debates on the Catiline Conspiracy, in the Roman Senate, B. C. 63, were reported in a brief form of writing (as acknowledged by Dr. Timothe Bright, the author of the first English system, in his dedication of his work to Queen Elizabeth), but *had actually imitated the characters of the ancient Roman shorthand writing in the construction of their alphabets.*

While there is not much, if any, trace of the Tironian *notae* to be found in Bright's "Characterie" (1588), which consists largely of arbitrary marks, the first alphabetic system, the "Stenographie" of John Willis (1602), contains unmistakable evidence that it was founded on the Roman stenographic characters.

When this theory became a conviction, I was interested to note that, with one exception, subsequent authors, for two hundred years, pursued the "bellwether" path of Willis, who had followed the zigzag "calf-path" made by Tiro more than seventeen centuries before! I do not think that in all history there is to be found a more striking illustration than this of the way man follows the beaten path of "well-established precedent."

The evolution of the art of shorthand through several centuries can be clearly traced. It is true that at times the art has strayed into by-paths or blind alleys; but nevertheless the student of shorthand history can find, century after century, evidences of gradual progress in some direction. Sometimes a principle which was condemned or ridiculed in the lifetime of its author received universal acceptance when revived later and applied in a more practical form.

"What is natural survives," and it was inevitable that, as time went on, the trend of shorthand construction would be toward principles which were in accord with the natural movements of the hand in writing; but the steps taken in that direction have been slow, hesitating, and laborious.

THE EVOLUTIONARY STEPS. The processes of evolution in shorthand, as I see them, were as follows:

The *first step* was the derivation of the characters of the Tironian notes from the majuscules, or capital letters, of the Latin writing of that time. The minuscule, or small letters that could be joined, and which were written in one direction—our current running hand—did not come into general use until the ninth century. As the majuscules of Latin are drawn in all directions, e.g., V, A, T, the shorthand characters derived from them were written in all directions—back slope, forward slope, and vertical.

The *second step* was the imitation of the Tironian notes by the early English authors, and, consequently, the adoption of the majuscule basis, which imposed upon the art for centuries the multi-sloped style of shorthand writing.

The *third step* was the very evident progress, through a series of early English systems, toward the expression of *each letter in the alphabet by a single character.* (The first alphabetic system, that of John Willis (1602), contained no less than nineteen *compound* forms for the twenty-six letters represented in the alphabet of that system.) This is probably the most clearly defined step of any.

An interesting illustration is the evolution of "f" and "v." In the Tironian *notae* the letter "v" was expressed by two strokes—a back-slope stroke and a forward up-stroke, in imitation of the Latin capital "V." Beginning with John Willis in 1602, the compound sign used by

Tiro for "v" was adopted by E. Willis (1618), Witt (1630), Dix (1633), Mawd (1635), Shelton (1641), Metcalfe (1645), Farthing (1654), and more than a score of other authors of early English systems, and continued in use for that very purpose, and in that very form, down to and including the noted system of James Weston, published in 1727. A forward step in the evolution of the form for "v" was taken in 1672 by William Mason, when he dropped the upward stroke and used only the single back-slope character. This was so brief and practical that it was adopted by the two most famous authors of the eighteenth century, John Byrom, and Samuel Taylor, as well as by Lewis, Floyd, Dodge, Gould, Hinton, Moat, and others. All these authors expressed *f* or *v by the same sign.*

Then, with Molineux's "Introduction to Byrom's Shorthand" (1802), we have still another evolutionary step. Molineux said: "The next consonant is *f* or *v,* the latter being in general represented by the same mark as *f;* although, occasionally, it may be useful to distinguish from the former by making the stroke a *little thicker.*" Molineux gave the same direction for distinguishing between *s* and *z,* "which were signified by one and the same line, the letter *z* being made a little thicker than the *s.*" William Harding, in his edition of the Taylor system (1823), published after the death of Taylor, adopted Molineux's expedient for distinguishing between *f* and *v* by shading the latter, and also the same method of distinction between *s* and *z,* which were previously written alike.

Isaac Pitman studied the Harding edition of Taylor, and in the first edition of his system in 1837, which was called "Stenographic Sound-Hand," he used the same signs as Harding for *f* and *v*—the straight back-slope character, written light for *f* and heavy for *v.* In a later edition he changed the form to a back-slope curve.

Another very interesting letter to trace through its various processes of evolution in the earlier systems is the letter *r.* Edmund Willis represented *r* by one of the script forms for that letter. As time went on, this was modified until it assumed the form of a straight upward stroke, with a little tick before it, resembling the check-mark used by bookkeepers. Even Isaac Pitman, in his first alphabet, used this check-mark sign for *r;* but he gave, as an *alternative,* the upward stroke without the tick. After a while it was found that the tick was unnecessary, and it was dropped.

The *fourth step* was the gradual acceptance of the principle of "writing by sound," and the provision of characters that rendered it possible to express the phonetic sounds. The author of the very first system of alphabetic shorthand, John Willis (1602), said: "It is to be observed that this art prescribeth the writing of words, not according to the orthography as they are written, but according to their sound as they are pronounced." As the alphabets of the early English systems were not arranged on a phonetic basis, since they provided characters for *c* (which is sounded as *k, could,* or *s, cease*), *q* (which is pronounced *kw*), *x* (which is pronounced *ks*), and did not provide characters for simple sounds like *sh, th, ch,* it was impossible to carry out the direction to write words "according to their sound." Most of the early authors recognized this, and contented themselves with directing the student to "omit silent letters." It was not until the end of the eighteenth and the beginning of the nineteenth centuries that the negative statement of the principle, "omit silent letters," was changed to the positive "write by sound," and that characters were provided which enabled the direction to be carried into effect— Holdsworth and Aldridge (1766), Conen de Prépéan (1816), Phinehas Bailey (1831), Towndrow (1835), Pitman (1837).

The *fifth step* was the arrangement of the consonantal characters according to their phonetic relationship: thus, *p, b, t, d,* etc.,—Holdsworth and Aldridge (1766), Conen de Prépéan, Byrom, Pitman, and others.

The *sixth step* was the founding of the characters of the alphabet partly upon modern cursive longhand forms instead of upon the ancient Roman capitals. Even the alphabet of John Willis (1602) took a hesitating step in this direction in the expression of *y* by a character that imitated the small *y* of current writing. Other authors extended the use of cursive characters to *r, h,* and other letters.

That forward running characters were more facile than back-slope characters was recognized early in the history of modern shorthand. This is shown by the fact that characters on the natural slope of writing, or with an onward movement, were given the preference in the representation of frequently occurring letters. One of the most noted and talented of shorthand authors, John Byrom, M. A., F. R. S., who taught his system to many distinguished people (among whom were John and Charles Wesley), for many years, though the system was not published until 1767, several years after his death, said: "The other *th* [a back-slope character], *by reason of our customary method of leaning the letters the contrary way in common writing, is not so readily made,"* etc.

The first system founded *wholly* upon a cursive basis was that of Simon Bordley (1787); but as it was buried in a formidable treatise called "Cadmus Britannicus," it escaped attention. It was not until 1802, when Richard Roe published "A new system of shorthand, in which legibility and brevity are secured upon the most natural principles, especially by the singular property of their sloping all one way according to habitual motion of the hand in common writing," that the cursive principle was stated boldly and definitely as a basic principle in shorthand construction.

But the new principle, as expounded by Roe, was almost foredoomed to failure. In the first place, the limitations of shorthand material, as known at that time, seemed to render the application of the principle utterly impracticable; in the second place, Roe's system, like most first ventures in a new direction, was a very crude production; in the third place, and most important of all, it was placed before the public at a time when the older geometric styles, after two hundred years of progression, had reached a high degree of development, and were being used by Thomas Gurney and others for professional reporting.

One can easily imagine that the shorthand authors and writers of that time viewed Roe's work in very much the same spirit as those who had developed the gas balloon to a high state of perfection regarded the theories of Langley, Wright, and others, who believed that it was possible to construct a "heavier-than-air" machine. Why waste time with "cranks" who held such preposterous notions?

But the *principle* enunciated by Roe did not die. In 1816, Thomas Oxley made an attempt to give effect to it; and a few years later the great Bavarian author, Franz Xavier Gabelsberger, produced a system based on the current hand, which either in its original form or in modifications of it, soon became almost universally used in Germany and all other European countries, with the exception of France and Spain. French writers have asserted that Gabelsberger derived his inspiration from Oxley's work, but this theory may be the outcome of national prejudice.

The style of writing in the German systems has a very involved and lengthy appearance; but it is, nevertheless, much more *fluent* than the stiff, geometric style. Gabelsberger described the writing in his system as consisting of "meandering loops and lines," and that description would apply to all other German systems, as they are founded on the principles laid down by the great Bavarian author. It is to this characteristic of the German systems that I attribute their failure to attain any real foothold among English-speaking people, who are accustomed to a style of writing, both in longhand and shorthand, in which there is greater simplicity of form than in Teutonic writing. Following the publication in England and America of adaptations to English of the French system of Duployé, an active propaganda was inaugurated in London and New York on behalf of adaptations of the German systems of Gabelsberger and Stolze; but it was without any practical results so far as the advancement of the German style of shorthand was concerned. It had one good result, however: It directed the attention of British and American shorthand writers to the success of systems founded on the cursive style of writing, as distinguished from the old angular and multi-sloped geometric styles. Incidentally, too, it brought into bold relief the popularity of shorthand and the high esteem in which it was held by educated people in Germany, as contrasted with the lack of interest in the subject in English-speaking countries, where a style of shorthand writing then prevailed which was not in harmony with natural movement. This concentrated attention on the problem of developing a style of shorthand combining the uniformity and fluency of movement of ordinary writing with simpler and clearer forms than those used in the German systems.

The *seventh step* was a very slow and halting one. It was towards the joining of vowels and consonants in the natural order in which they occur in a word. The expression of vowels by strokes in the earlier systems was so clumsy that, in seeking relief from the burden of their expression, it is not surprising that some of the early shorthand authors (Samuel Taylor, for example) went to the other extreme of expressing *any* vowel by a dot. Others attempted to give a more definite expression by placing dots, "commas," or dashes in various positions alongside the consonants; but in practice most of the vowels were omitted. In those leisurely days, when shorthand was studied for the most part by highly educated and studious people as a useful accomplishment for reporting sermons and public addresses, or was studied for professional reporting purposes over a series of years, the absence of vowels was not so keenly felt as in our day. After much practice, well-educated people and trained reporters could tell almost instinctively when it was wise to insert a vowel, or, if a vowel was omitted, they could usually determine from the context, or from memory, what the word should be, even when the "consonantal skeleton" might represent a dozen words. In more recent times, when shorthand was studied for the most part by very young people for use in business offices, the ridiculous mistakes made through the absence of vowels in the shorthand forms emphasized the importance of a more adequate representation of them. Young people have not the education, discrimination, or maturity of judgment, necessary to "guess" correctly which word out of a possible dozen or more represented by the same "consonantal skeleton" was dictated. It was this factor, more than any other, which gave vitality to the demand in recent years for a more definite expression of the vowels.

The history of vowel representation might be summarized as follows:

Under *Disjoined Vowels* we might trace the use of the disjoined signs for vowels, beginning with the dot for "i" in Rich, then the use of "commas" as well as dots, the gradual substitution of dashes for "commas"; the placing of dots in different position with relation to the consonants— at first in five positions, later reduced by Byrom to three; the formulation of rules governing the use of these dots and dashes before and after consonants; and the extension of the phonetic principle to the dots and dashes expressing the vowels and diphthongs.

Under *Vowel Indication* we might begin with Tiro's method of writing the consonant characters at different angles to express vowels, and trace the evolution of the expedient through Gurney's "vowel-modes" (adopted, in part, by Professor Everett) through Pitman's method of indicating, in the case of a few characters, *where* a vowel *occurred,* by writing some letters upward to show that a vowel followed it, and other strokes downward to show that a vowel preceded it; through Melville Bell to Pocknell, Valpy, Browne, and others, who extended this expedient to *all* consonants. But it is hardly necessary to do this, as all the so-called "vowel indication" systems have passed away. None of them did more than indicate *where* a vowel occurred; and any method which does not indicate not only where a vowel occurs, but *what* the vowel is—or at least approximately what it is—has no possible chance of consideration in these times.

Another form of "vowel-indication" was by writing words in position. As explained in a previous chapter, the Pitmanic systems placed words in three positions, each position "indicating" that one of about five vowels occurred somewhere in the word. This was extended to *five* positions by J. George Cross (1877) and was imitated by a number of authors— McKee, Byrne, Chartier.

Under *Joined Vowels* we might trace the evolution of joined-vowel systems from stroke forms, beginning with Tiro, on through Willis and others; the gradual substitution of simpler forms, beginning with the use of the circle by Blanchard in 1786, until the adoption of the circles, hooks and loops, by Conen de Prépéan (1805), Duployé, and others, as the most facile and logical material for the expression of the vowels; and, later, the use of the circles, hooks, and loops for the expression of the vowels in accordance with the *facility-value of the material and the frequency-value of the vowels represented.*

The *eighth step* was in the direction of the use of characters of the one thickness. The difficulty of finding material to express the letters without resorting to compound forms suggested the use of characters of varying degrees of thickness. When shading was first introduced, it was in harmony with the style of longhand writing then in vogue, as may be seen from the specimens of longhand writing of that period. As mere artistic productions, some of these specimens are a delight to the eye, with the broad, sweeping, shaded strokes, which could be readily and artistically executed by the quill pens then in use. In that leisurely age such decorative specimens of ordinary writing naturally suggested the use of shading for shorthand characters; but the demand for rapidity in more modern times relegated the ornate shaded style of writing to the discard. As explained in a previous chapter, the apparent gains obtained by the use of shading in shorthand were purely illusory, as they were more than counterbalanced by the losses.

The *ninth step* is the most recent of all, and it has not yet received the attention and appreciation that will undoubtedly be given it in years to come. It is the principle of founding the writing not only on the uniform slope of ordinary writing, but upon the curvilinear motion of longhand, as opposed to the angular style of writing. As this has been treated somewhat fully in one of the chapters of this book, it is not necessary to say more about it here.

WHY CERTAIN SYSTEMS FAILED. It is my belief that many authors of systems published in the past fifty years failed to attain greater success than they did because they lacked a *controlling ideal.* They had in view, for example, the elimination of shading, or of position writing, or possibly both; or it may have been the inclusion of the vowels in the outline, or the slope-of-longhand theory—or a combination of any two of these. Whatever it was, they concentrated on *one* or *two* phases of the subject without having a broad conception of the entire problem. They had not the definite ideal of constructing a system based *through-out* on a close analysis of those easy, natural movements which the experience of mankind has embodied in our beautiful longhand writing. None of them, indeed, started from the premise that our ordinary writing in all its features was the natural basis of a briefer form of writing. I speak understandingly and sympathetically about this because at the time of my own early efforts at shorthand construction I had not formulated that guiding principle.

Probably the sequence of the mental operations of many authors ran something like this: "I believe in joined vowels. That is a natural, logical principle; therefore joined vowels there shall be in the system I am going to construct. But in introducing joined vowels there may be a loss in brevity of form—what can I do to offset that?"

Then the answer suggested itself: "Why not extend the use of shading, of position writing, or of characters of different lengths? These expedients can stand a little more pressure on them."

The result of this reasoning was that most of these systems contain one or two *natural* principles on which great emphasis is placed; but the gain in this respect is offset, and sometimes more than offset, by the extension of certain *unnatural* features.

Keeping this guiding principle in mind—that the ideal shorthand system should be "the distilled essence of our common calligraphy," as someone expressed it,—we can now understand why so many systems published in modern times failed to attain greater success. They failed because:

1. They eliminated but *one* or *two* of the unnatural features found in the older systems, and retained all the others.

2. While eliminating one or two unnatural features, some of them extended the use of other unnatural features far beyond the limitations imposed in the older systems.

CONCLUSION. After I had completed the preceding chapters of this book, in which the basic principles of the system had been fully explained, an event occurred which inclined me to "scrap" the entire manuscript. It was the winning of the Shorthand Championship by Albert Schneider—at the age of twenty. The old saying, "The proof of the pudding is in the eating," and the maxim, "The public is educated quickly by events, slowly by arguments," came to mind. I said, "Why should I print a book setting forth an elaborate presentation of the scientific principles on which Gregg Shorthand was built, when the soundness of those principles has been placed beyond all reasonable controversy by the actual achievements of its writers."

But the book has been written, and as I dislike to think that it has been a needless expenditure of time and labor, I am sending it forth. It may serve a useful purpose in furnishing the shorthand historian of the future with data on which to base a history in which the evolutionary principles may be traced—as distinguished from the mere cataloguing of the names and works of the various shorthand authors, as is the case with most of the histories that have appeared in the past. It may, too, prove of service to the advocates of the system in giving reasons for the faith within them.

4

JOHN ROBERT GREGG, THE TEACHER

In addition to the material given in the first three parts in this book, Gregg's thinking about shorthand may be found scattered through his rare public speeches and in his occasional writings—prefaces to his textbooks and the like. In this part some of the nuggets have been mined from these writings and given in appropriate groupings with enough comment to explain the context from which they are taken. Excerpts are also given from the two small books of Gregg's writing and speaking, *The Teaching of Shorthand* and *The Use of the Blackboard in Teaching Shorthand*. These volumes are out of print; but some of this material should be preserved, even though much of it is no longer timely.

Thoughts on the Writing and Teaching of Shorthand

GREGG was a great innovator in both shorthand principles and shorthand teaching methods. It is difficult to realize this today, because most of his innovations have become so much a part of our shorthand writing and teaching that they are taken for granted. The digest of his *Basic Principles of Gregg Shorthand,* given as Part 3 of this book, covers his innovations in shorthand principles, which need not be repeated here.

The innovations in methods were numerous and radical. Many of them ran counter to the fixed ideas of the teachers of other, very different, shorthand systems of the time. As the inventor himself wrote [5:457] [1] in 1931, when reviewing the various editions of Gregg Shorthand:

> All the presentations of the system marked a radical change from the accepted methods of presenting or teaching shorthand. One reason for this is the fact that the author was a *teacher* of shorthand, while most authors of shorthand have not been teachers. As a *teacher,* he understood the conditions under which shorthand has to be taught and had due appreciation of the time and attention that must be given to other subjects. Even the language in which the instruction was given was adapted to all conditions and to all types of students.

He was indeed a teacher, a great teacher, as those who have seen him teach will testify. Because he was one of those rare "born teachers," he never wrote much about methods of teaching. He always felt that the teacher should know by instinct how to teach. Also, as he wrote [23:iii] in 1936:

> One of the most fascinating things about "the lithe and noble art of brief writing" is the infinite variety of methods that can be adopted in teaching it. For this reason I have always maintained a receptive attitude toward new methods of handling the subject. After all, the *system* is my main

[1] Instead of using footnotes to indicate references, bracketed figures, like [5:457], have been used. The bracketed figures in this reference indicate that the work referred to is listed as the numbered item 5 in the "Sources" at the end of this part and that the page referred to is page 457.

interest, and any method that promised to contribute to the attainment of better results in teaching it was deserving of consideration.

Nevertheless, his own great gifts as a natural teacher greatly influenced the teaching of shorthand through the presentation of his shorthand system in the textbooks he wrote. Even the best teacher cannot teach well from a poorly arranged shorthand textbook. From the beginning, Gregg knew that shorthand should be taught as a skill or an art rather than as a science. He liked to quote the saying of the German shorthand inventor who distinguished between the science of shorthand and the art of shorthand writing. In the Preface to the Anniversary Edition of Gregg Shorthand in 1929, he wrote [9:iii]:

> Anyone who examines the shorthand textbooks of the last three centuries will be impressed with the fact that they have reflected the uses to which shorthand was put at the time the books were written.
> The pedagogy of shorthand has changed as radically as the content of the textbooks. Up to the time Gregg Shorthand was introduced, the conventional pedagogy was to teach the theory of a system as a whole before attempting to apply the theory in the actual writing of connected matter. While the system would undoubtedly have made its way into public favor by its own inherent strength, we believe that its success and progress throughout the world have been hastened enormously by the teachability of its textbooks.
> In keeping with the progress in business and in education, the Gregg Manual was revised [several times]. Each revision marked a step forward in simplifying and popularizing the study of shorthand. Each revision has placed increasing emphasis upon the desirability of teaching shorthand as a *skill subject* from the beginning and throughout the entire course. This method enables the teacher to direct the maximum of effort toward the training of the student in actual facility in writing and the minimum of effort to expositions of rules and principles.

In the Preface to the 1902 edition, the inventor comments on the new feature that had great influence on teaching methods—the introduction of phrasing in the first lesson. This now seems natural to all shorthand teachers. In the early writings on the teaching of shorthand, however, there were many articles on the difficulties of teaching shorthand phrasing. The explanation is given in this excerpt [7:ix]:

An important innovation is the introduction of phrase-writing from the very first lesson. It has been the custom to postpone phrase-writing until the principles of shorthand have been mastered; but all teachers know that when a student has acquired a habit of writing words separately—words that should naturally be joined—it is extremely difficult for him to afterwards obtain an easy command of phrase-writing. By using simple phrases from the beginning of the study, the student easily acquires a habit of joining words and requires little special instruction in that very important part of the study.

Many years later, in 1931, Gregg mentioned this change, which now seems to us so commonplace, like so many of those that came first from his fertile genius [5:456]:

In the "Revised Edition" (July 2, 1902), phrases were introduced in the First Lesson, and this was then regarded as a daring innovation!

Earlier innovations made by the young genius are immediately apparent upon a comparison of his first 1888 edition with the other shorthand textbooks then available. The first thing that is noticeable is the complete absence of any of the extensive phonetic preparation that was common in 1888. The books of that time explained at length about explodents, labials, fricatives, and dentals. Gregg's book just began to teach shorthand. As he said in 1902, referring to his earlier books [7:vii]:

The instruction was given in simple language, free from the long pedantic discussions about "continuants, explodents, fricatives, coalescents, etc.," which were so dear to the hearts of the old style books.

The shorthand systems of 1888 were presented by means of a complicated structure of elaborate rules, rules that were, for the most part, necessary for the writing of the difficult systems then in vogue. In the first edition of Gregg Shorthand, in 1888, there is not a single rule. There are only two suggestions for abbreviating, but no rules for joining strokes. A printed key was given for all the shorthand in that first edition.

That little book was fifty years ahead of the times in methods. The teachers of that day, accustomed to complicated systems that required intricate verbalized rules, and unaccustomed to the use of the key to the shorthand, demanded rules and demanded the abolition of the key.

The inventor's chief problem was to sell his system. He could not afford, as he often told this writer, to complicate that problem by an insistence on methods to which the teachers were not accustomed.

Similarly, the first edition of 1888 used the simplest shorthand outlines, outlines that involved the least learning or memory difficulty. The teachers of other systems, systems that had achieved apparent brevity of outline by complicated rules and a heavy memory load, insisted that the Gregg outlines looked too long. The inventor wisely gave in to these objections, in order to introduce the system, with the knowledge that the teachers would eventually become accustomed to the cursive style of shorthand writing and that the system could then be returned to its original simplicity.

With this background, it is doubly interesting to read the Preface to the very rare 1901 British edition of what was then called *Gregg's Shorthand*. This was published in Stratford-on-Avon. The Preface also shows the tremendous conviction and enthusiasm of the 34-year-old inventor who has, as he says, "the conscious power that comes from successful achievement." The first paragraph of the following excerpt has a very familiar ring to this writer, who so often heard Gregg say these things with profound sincerity in his voice. This writer can also testify to the sincerity of Gregg's promise to continue to promote the use of Gregg Shorthand in the British Isles "even at a considerable loss." To our own personal knowledge, he did continue the vigorous promotion of the system in the British Isles until his death in 1948, and every year "at a considerable loss." He never drew a penny of profit from it and continued it for the reasons sincerely stated in the first paragraph below [10:iv]:

> Our work here has grown to immense proportions, and it is not of much moment to us whether the business done with the old country is profitable or not. We would be glad to see it yield a revenue; but in any event we intend to continue it, even at a considerable loss, because we believe in the system as an educational reform which must eventually triumph. Remembering our own early struggles with complicated methods, we are resolved, at whatever sacrifice of time and money, to relieve the needless burdens imposed upon shorthand students of Great Britain and Ireland. This

was the spirit which animated us in our early struggles against a hidebound conservatism and prejudice, and we have lost none of our enthusiasm for the cause, while we have gained experience and the conscious power that comes from successful achievement.

Looking back to those early days, we can now see that the greatest element of weakness in the movement, next to the faulty textbooks then used, was the policy of advocating the system on the ground of SIMPLICITY. That it is a simple system cannot be denied, but simplicity is the least of its merits. Its success in this country was delayed for a time by the same policy, as the great commercial training schools of America are conducted on purely business principles, and a simple system, at first sight, naturally suggested a shorter course of instruction and a decreased revenue. It was only when it had been repeatedly demonstrated that better average results and a higher standard of competency could be attained by the use of the Gregg system that its adoption became imperative and it swept through the country.

The lesson of this is clear: Rely absolutely upon the actual results accomplished by your students, and do not advocate the system as a simple shorthand. If this course is steadily pursued by our teachers, the intrinsic merits of Gregg Shorthand and that sturdy adherence to what they believe to be for the public welfare, which is a distinguishing characteristic of the British people, may be relied upon to ensure its almost universal adoption in the near future.

The simplicity of the system was and still is one of its finest features. It is that simplicity that enables Gregg Shorthand to give such good results in so brief a time, and the inventor never forgot that fact. At the time of his death in 1948, he was engaged in the preparation of the Gregg Shorthand Simplified series that appeared in 1949, and he had been working on it for more than ten years.

As the inventor reminds us in the next excerpt, written in 1931, the simplicity of the system was one of his chief sources of pride. In this excerpt he quotes from his 1888 Preface, in which the new system is described as "simple, rapid, and perfectly legible." Notice that the boy of twenty who wrote that first Preface placed the word "simple" first in the list of merits of his new system and the man of sixty-four, writing forty-four years later, comes back again to the simplicity of the system, although thirty years earlier he had advised the British advocates of the system, for practical reasons, not to stress simplicity.

Throughout his life he clung to the dream of a "phonetic hand-writing." In 1935 he did issue a privately printed "phonetic hand-writing" for experimental purposes. It was not, however, until 1960 that *Gregg Notehand* was finally published and became an immediate success as the "phonetic handwriting" of which the inventor dreamed in 1888.

The reference in the first sentence of the excerpt to "the division of the system into two parts" refers to the fact that in 1888 the system was published in two small booklets. The article from which this excerpt is taken was written in 1931 as a backward look over the various editions of the *Gregg Shorthand Manual* at that time [5:456]:

> To understand the division of the system into two parts, the purpose of the author must be kept in mind, as expressed in the first sentence of the preface of the first edition:
>
> "A great and increasing demand for a simple, rapid, and perfectly legible phonetic handwriting for general use has led to the invention of Light-Line Phonography." The purpose, it will be seen, was not so much the production of a superior system of shorthand for commercial or reporting purposes as a simplified form of brief writing *"for general use."* Hence the first pamphlet was intended for that purpose, and the second pamphlet was intended to provide abbreviations for those who desired to use shorthand for business or reporting work.
>
> While it is true that the closing paragraph of the preface declared that it was not merely a simple system but one "rapid enough to reproduce verbatim the fastest oratory," the dominant thought was "a shorthand for general use." I clung to that ideal tenaciously until it became clear that the only way in which I could earn a livelihood was by teaching shorthand for business purposes. In yielding to this necessity, I did so with the thought that when the system had demonstrated its superiority for commercial work and reporting, its value would be more readily recognized as a time- and labor-saving accomplishment.
>
> Through all the subsequent years, absorbed and enmeshed as I have been with the details of a constantly expanding movement and organization, I have looked forward to the time when it would be possible to return to my original purpose by inaugurating a campaign for the use of shorthand by everybody who had much writing to do. It has been a source of profound regret to me that time after time the pressure of other things has resulted in

the postponement of such a campaign. It will come some day! The ever-increasing pressure of the times will render it inevitable.

In line with the last two excerpts was Gregg's constant insistence that the study of shorthand should be a pleasure, that it should be made simple and easy. In the 1901 Preface he speaks of his desire "to relieve the needless burdens imposed upon the shorthand student." In 1893, before he had come to this country for the first time, he wrote [15:12]:

> Above all things, the student should keep in mind that the study of Light-Line [as Gregg Shorthand was then known] should be a pleasure and not a drudgery. The most common error is to forget that shorthand writing is more of a mental than a mechanical process, and that if the writer can "think out" the correct outline rapidly enough, he will find little or no difficulty in transferring it to paper. . . . If it is possible, you should study in a room by yourself, so that you can repeat each word aloud as you write it. . . .

In this one brief paragraph he covered many points of his teaching philosophy. The most important point is the realization that "shorthand writing is more of a mental than a mechanical process." We shall revert to this later. For the moment, let us look at another excerpt expressing Gregg's feeling that the study of shorthand should be "a perfect joy." When he wrote the next paragraph in 1916, he was forty-nine years old but had obviously lost none of his radiant enthusiasm for shorthand. This paragraph is almost poetry, so intense is his enthusiasm. Reading this paragraph, it is possible to understand the great persuasiveness that he had when talking about shorthand in general, and his own system in particular. Few could resist him. This eloquent passage comes from the Preface to the 1916 edition, issued just as Gregg Shorthand was taught in as many schools as all other systems combined [8:xiii]:

> Success in any study depends largely upon the *interest* taken in the subject by the student. This being the case, we earnestly hope that you will realize at the very outset that shorthand can be made an intensely fascinating study. Cultivate a love for it. Think of it as the highest form of writing, which in itself is the greatest invention of man. Be

proud that you can record the language in its graceful lines and curves. Aim constantly to acquire artistic skill in executing these lines and curves. You *can,* if you *will,* make the study of shorthand a perfect joy instead of a task. Its possession has been coveted by the wisest of men and women, for it is not only a practical instrument in commercial work, but a much prized and valuable accomplishment and a means of mental culture.

Gregg's fundamental shorthand philosophy, shared by very few at the time he published his system in 1888, is succinctly expressed in the sentence already quoted [15:12]:

> The most common error is to forget that shorthand is more of a mental than a mechanical process, and that if the writer can "think out" the correct outline rapidly enough, he will find little or no difficulty in transferring it to paper.

Gregg always regretted the pressures that compelled him to introduce into his system complications that he knew to be unnecessary, but without which he could not hope to persuade the teachers of that time to use the system. These complications were all directed toward the formation of shorter outlines. He knew, and constantly said in private, that the outline that appeared shortest to the eye or the hand was not usually the best or easiest outline for the shorthand writer. He often quoted the letter he received in 1885 from a French shorthand author and reporter [22:136]:

> Suppose a man were to dictate the number 1,634,725. And suppose that number is equal to 5^9. You will write much faster 1,634,725 in full than 5^9, which looks much shorter. Why so? It is evident. Yet, everyone will believe that 5^9 is more expeditious for the dictatee than 1,634,725. . . . The principle applies to shorthand. People who fancy that by dint of shortening the outlines they will gain speed make a heavy mistake. As a rule, they lose time.

This brings to mind a favorite story that Gregg told many times when speaking to groups of shorthand students or teachers. According to the story, a young man training to become a shorthand reporter learned a fine shortcut for *Plenipotentiary of the Almighty.* He practiced this phrase many times during his lifetime but never had a chance to use it, even though he did report many sermons. Finally, the day before he was to retire, he took a sermon in which the preacher did say *Plenipotentiary of the Almighty*. He was taken aback by hearing this favorite phrase for the first time after all these years and wrote the words out in full before he could stop to think of the phrase.

That story never failed to bring a laugh from the audience. Like so many facetious stories, however, it contains a profound truth. The best shorthand outline is the one that comes most readily to the mind. The inventor's realization of this fact is really the basis for the great success of Gregg Shorthand. In the five years during which he worked on the construction of his system, he constantly bore in mind the necessity for simplicity, for relieving the mind at the expense of the hand.

An excellent example of his understanding of this principle is his struggle to eliminate "position writing" from his system. Most of the systems in current use in England in the nineteenth century required that a shorthand outline be written above the line, on the line, or through the line to indicate certain vowels or consonants. It is an alluring device for the shorthand inventor who can thus solve some difficult problem easily.

Gregg continued the battle until he was able to eliminate position writing altogether, and all his life he continued to oppose any mention of position writing in the teaching of Gregg Shorthand. As he was so fond of saying, when the matter would be brought up in a discussion by teachers who insisted that the Gregg outlines should be written in some accurate relation to the ruled line in the notebook: "Don't worry about where the outline comes on the line. Tell your pupils that at 100 words a minute they are lucky to get the outlines on the page, let alone on the line!"

This genial statement of the evils of line placement or position writing dates from his later years. In 1888, as a young man of twenty, in his first edition, he wrote this scathing denunciation of position writing [13:4]:

> This, one of the chief stumbling blocks to the shorthand student, is nowhere to be found in Light-Line Phonography [as Gregg Shorthand was first called]. Like shading, this principle is destructive to lineality and phraseography, and is a constant source of embarrassment if applied, and of illegibility if neglected. Light-Line Phonography, like the ordinary longhand, may be written on unruled paper, and in one straight line.

Gregg never believed in the correction of the learner's shorthand exercises. As subsequent psychological research has proved, he was right in feeling that the correction of papers did not benefit the pupil and only wore out the teacher needlessly. Further, he knew that the correction of the papers brought about hesitations in the pupil's shorthand writing because it caused the pupil to think about the outlines; it violated the first principle of Gregg Shorthand: simplicity.

In writing the obituary notice of one of the great shorthand teachers of the early decades of this century, Gregg said [12:603-604]:

> We learned that once or twice a week she took a suitcase filled with notebooks home with her, even after night school, and sometimes stayed up until two or three o'clock in the morning correcting them in red ink. We remonstrated with her without avail.
>
> It was about this time that we gave a talk to teachers about the folly of "committing suicide by the red ink route." Miss Dixon knew very well that we had her in mind, but she merely smiled and continued using up bottles of red ink. She insisted that it was absolutely necessary to the success of her students. When we argued that such work entailed a severe drain on her physical strength which, if continued, would inevitably result in poorer work in the classroom, she smiled and said, "No, Mr. Gregg, you know that I love to do it, and anything we love to do does not tire us."

Gregg knew that because of the simplicity of his system it was not necessary to check each slight deviation from the textbook outline, as had been necessary in the older and more complicated systems. Many times, in his own shorthand writing, he would use an outline that was not the textbook outline at the time. Sometimes this writer would call his attention to such an outline, in fun. Gregg's reply was always the same: "You can read it, can't you?"

Often, when teachers would press the matter and would want a strict ruling that "this outline is right and that outline is wrong," he would say: "A correct outline is any outline that may be correctly transcribed."

This attitude toward the shorthand outlines led to an aversion to the teaching of rules and the discussion of technical points and correction of shorthand papers. He never could understand why teachers seemed to place so much importance on rules, because in his own teaching he paid very little attention to them. In 1924 he said [14:ii]:

It is, I believe, unnecessary for me to explain that it has been a guiding principle in the preparation of the textbooks of the system to state the rules and principles as simply as I know how. Indeed, I believe that the illustrations which follow each rule in the *Manual* are of much greater value in impressing the rule on the minds of the students than the mere *wording* of the rule.

Some years ago, in an address to young teachers, I warned them against an epidemic of what I termed short-hand technicitis" which appeared to be spreading all over the country at that time. By that expression I meant elaborate explanations of each rule and of every possible application or modification of the rule. Such detailed explanations are not only confusing to the student but are a source of discouragement. The young student will attain a better knowledge of the practical application of the rules, and greater skill in the execution of the forms, by actually writing and reading a great variety of words in which the rule is applied than he will from oral explanations of it.

One of the most successful teachers I have known put my ideas very well when he said, "In presenting a lesson, teach the 'high spots' only—the rest will be made clear in practice."

He repeated this same thought even more emphatically [6:276-277] fifteen years later, in 1939. Notice that his suggestion is "to keep the students so busy writing and reading that they will not waste time on things that are of no real importance."

One great obstacle to the attainment of high speed is the placing of too much emphasis on minor points of theory. This is not so prevalent as it was a few years ago, but it still exists. At one time it was a real menace, so much so that I coined a phrase for it, "shorthand technicitis," and wrote many articles about it. . . . The thing to do is to keep the students so busy writing and reading that they will not waste time on things that are of no real importance. As one very successful teacher said, "In teaching the principles and giving word-building drills, I aim to hit the 'high spots' only. The rest will be absorbed by writing and reading."

Gregg often expressed the same thought in his talks by saying that he believed in teaching "once over lightly; then dictate, dictate, dictate."

In this connection he used to like to tell the story of a large

American city that adopted Gregg Shorthand on very short notice. The teachers had been teaching another system and suddenly had to begin to teach Gregg Shorthand. The first year they achieved splendid shorthand results, and everybody was very happy with the new system. The second year the results were not very good, and the third year they were terrible. Gregg himself went to visit the classes to determine the cause of the poor results. After watching the teachers and talking with them, he found the cause of the trouble.

The first year, the teachers were learning the system day by day with the pupils. Their knowledge of Gregg Shorthand was so slight that they feared questions from the class. They knew that any question that might be asked would be difficult for them to answer. Therefore, as one teacher told Gregg: "Every time a pupil looked up, I would begin to dictate, *Dear Sir,* to prevent him from asking some question that I might not be able to answer." The second year, the teachers knew the system better and did not hesitate to answer questions. But the third year, they all knew Gregg Shorthand very well indeed, and they invited questions. Each year, as the discussion increased and the dictation decreased, the results became worse and worse. Gregg used to call that the "Dear Sir method" of teaching shorthand. This was an actual experience, of which this writer had personal knowledge. It was not just a story to illustrate the point he makes in the last two excerpts.

He often said in meetings and in informal discussion: "The only really worthwhile activity that goes on in the shorthand classroom is the reading and writing of shorthand. Anything else is usually a waste of time." That was his tactful way of saying that the teacher's explanations and discussions of rules are better omitted.

One of the most interesting of the inventor's comments on the subject of the teaching of rules happened to appear under the name of this writer. In 1935, when the manuscript of *The Teaching of Gregg Shorthand by the Functional Method* was completed, the inventor was kind enough to revise it before it went to the printer. Most of the changes he made consisted of the improvement of a sentence here and there. He did, however, insert two complete paragraphs [24:42] in his own shorthand notes on the margin of the manuscript. They were incorporated into the manuscript without change, as he wrote them:

> It will be obvious to any teacher that nearly all the rules in Gregg Shorthand governing the formation of outlines are so easy and natural that when the student sees them applied

in writing words—when his mind is stocked with mental pictures of the various combinations through reading shorthand—he will not think of writing them otherwise. It is only when he is trying to construct words from the alphabetic forms without having a mental picture of how shorthand forms are really written that he gropes blindly, hesitatingly, in putting the characters together. Stock his mind with enough pictures of the shorthand forms, and this blind groping will disappear, and rule-teaching will be rendered unnecessary. In the Functional Method, the almost revolutionary treatment of minimizing the rules in the Anniversary Edition of the Gregg Shorthand Manual is just pushed to its logical conclusion.

There are comparatively few joinings in shorthand; once the student has read the outlines for a number of words in which the circle is placed outside an angle, he will instinctively and automatically place the circle outside the angle—usually it will not occur to him that it might be written in any other way.

No better statement was ever made of the case against the rule teaching than that. In the following year Gregg wrote a foreword to the first edition of the *Functional Method Manual*. In that foreword he quotes from his preface to his 1929 Manual [23:iv]:

All the editions of our Manual have been marked by a trend toward greater simplicity in the presentation of the rules until, in the Anniversary Edition, the rules were almost eliminated, many of them being put in the form of explanatory footnotes. As the Preface to the Anniversary Edition said:

Each revision marked a step forward in simplifying and popularizing the study of shorthand. Each revision has placed increasing emphasis upon the desirability of teaching shorthand as a *skill subject* from the beginning and throughout the entire course. The method enables the teacher to direct the maximum of effort toward the training of the student in actual facility in writing and the minimum of effort to expositions of rules and principles.

In the Functional Method, Mr. Leslie has pushed two basic principles in my shorthand philosophy, if I may so term it, to their utmost limit. One of these is that of minimizing rule teaching and placing the emphasis on reading and writing shorthand. The Functional Method does not merely minimize the teaching of rules—it abolishes the study of rules. The other principle is that at the beginning a student should not be asked to write anything in shorthand until he has a clear mental picture of what he is to write. In the Functional Method this Reading Approach is carried far beyond anything I attempted or contemplated.

Twenty years earlier, in 1917, Gregg gave, in the Preface to his *Gregg Speed Studies,* a persuasive explanation of the reason why "the best results are obtained through the reading of shorthand." In reading this 1917 Preface, however, it must be remembered that his very first textbook, in 1888, had been an all-shorthand text, with a key, in type, for the shorthand. Every word that he wrote in 1917 holds true today. He said then [11:iii-iv]:

An examination of the book will, I believe, disclose many notable contributions to the pedagogy of shorthand; but the two outstanding features are:

First, the presentation of practice material *in its shorthand form* instead of in print as is done in most dictation books.

Second, the development of a large and varied writing vocabulary through the unique plan of incorporating *vocabulary drills* with the work in dictation.

The first of these features can hardly be overemphasized. Much observation in teaching shorthand has convinced me that the best results are obtained through the reading of shorthand. The reasons may be summarized briefly:

1. The student is more interested in reading shorthand than in reading print, and interest in a subject is of the first importance in securing results.

2. As he may be called upon to read the shorthand notes at any point in the assignment, he will naturally give more time to preparing himself to read fluently.

3. In doing this, he familiarizes himself with the correct forms for words and phrases, and every new form makes a vivid impression on his mind.

4. The visual impression of the outline secured through reading enables him to write it readily when the matter is dictated to him. This inspires confidence, which is an important factor in the development of skill.

5. Through reading shorthand that has actually been written (not drawn by rule and compass), he learns the changes in length, slant, curvature, etc., which outlines undergo in various joinings, and he becomes impressed with the importance of absolute accuracy.

6. In reading from his own notes, he is helped, to a certain extent, by memory of the subject matter and even of the actual dictation; but in reading shorthand that has not been dictated to him, he must depend entirely upon his knowledge of the system and of the forms. This stimulates his mind to greater alertness and leads to much greater fluency in reading his own notes.

7. The student trained in this way finds shorthand a real medium of communication, and learns the application of the word-building principles through almost effortless absorption. In any art, imitation plays an important part. It is fully utilized by this plan.

It is interesting to notice in the last paragraph of the previous excerpt the restatement of Gregg's oft-repeated conviction that the student trained by the use of reading material in shorthand "learns the application of the word-building principles through almost effortless absorption." Again, twenty-two years later, this opinion is repeated in the Preface to the 1929 Anniversary Edition [9:iii]:

Devote much time to reading well-written shorthand. By reading a great deal of well-written shorthand, you will become not only a fluent reader, but you will enlarge your writing vocabulary. Unconsciously you will imitate in your own work the easy execution of the forms shown in the printed plates. All expert writers have devoted much time to reading shorthand.

In 1902 he wrote in the Preface to the revised *Gregg Shorthand Manual* of that year [7:ix]:

The shorthand forms were reproduced by photo-engraving from my shorthand notes. This method does not give the exactness of form secured by having the outlines drawn by rule and compass, but I believe it is the better plan for the reason that it presents shorthand as *actually written*. Shorthand characters drawn by a draftsman with mechanical precision are ungraceful and lifeless, while skillfully written notes convey an impression of artistic ease of execution that is a constant source of inspiration and encouragement to the student. The slight deviations in the length or shape of the characters so written will familiarize him with the variations to which all written shorthand is subject, and will increase his ability in reading.

In the Foreword to the 1936 *Functional Method Manual,* Gregg reminded the shorthand teacher that it is necessary to let the shorthand learner see the outlines *in motion.* The reading and copying of the shorthand in the textbook will give the learner most of the help he needs. As Gregg says, however, "form is the result of movement." From the very first day of shorthand instruction, the learners should see the teacher write shorthand on the blackboard in order that they may assimilate the movement by which the forms are produced. Gregg did not mean that the teacher should explain that movement—simply demonstrate.

Gregg often said, semihumorously, that he could go into a shorthand classroom just before the bell rang for the end of the period and tell how good the teacher was by looking at the amount of shorthand on the blackboard. There is very little exaggeration in this statement. The same thought is expressed more formally in this excerpt [23:v]:

> The clear visualization of the forms before writing them is important in the beginning, but there comes a time when mere visualization of the forms will not convey to the student the easy, rapid manner in which the forms and combinations are written by experts. As I said in the first chapter of *The Use of the Blackboard in Teaching Shorthand:*
>
> > Textbook illustrations go much farther in real teaching than any amount of printed description. But they cannot go so far as the teacher goes in his illustrations on the board. The teacher can demonstrate movement, which is just as important as form, because form is the result of movement. This the textbook illustration cannot give.

Another brief paragraph from *The Use of the Blackboard in Teaching Shorthand* recapitulates several of the points made in previous excerpts, and especially his constant emphasis on the desirability of little talking and much practicing during the shorthand period [20:93]:

> Let the blackboard do its full share of the work. Trust it. Don't do all the talking. The chalk outlines themselves are eloquent. They leave for the teacher's utterance only those brief remarks which drive each point home. And the points to be driven home will gain added force because of that very saving of words.

Another point on which Gregg felt strongly was emphasized in the Preface to the 1929 Anniversary Edition, in which he stresses that "scientifically graded connected matter has supplanted the isolated form." Putting the following excerpt together with the previous ones, it is clear that the inventor strongly felt that shorthand practice should be from well-written shorthand plates rather than from type, should be from connected matter rather than from lists of isolated words, and that the learner should absorb the principles of word-building from this type of practice work without any necessity for rule teaching [9:xiii]:

> In shorthand it is not sufficient to *know* how to write a word—you must not only know the form but be able to write it quickly. Hence the necessity for much *repetition practice* in writing the forms.
>
> Most of this repetition practice should be on the forms as they occur naturally in connected matter . . . scientifically graded connected matter has supplanted the isolated form.

A few excerpts concerning shorthand penmanship should, perhaps, be clarified by explaining what Gregg meant by shorthand penmanship. As a careful reading of these excerpts will show, and as we know by familiarity with his thinking over a long period of years, shorthand penmanship meant *fluency* to him. He was a friend and contemporary of A. N. Palmer, who did so much to introduce the idea of fluency into longhand penmanship. Both men understood that fluent, legible writing is much more valuable to the writer than beautiful but slow writing. His comments in these excerpts must be read in the light of the custom of the day. In 1899 students were trained to write slowly and carefully. Gregg insisted that they should be allowed and encouraged to write fluently from the beginning, even though the accuracy of form might suffer somewhat. As he said [2:46]:

> The danger is that if the student has impressed upon him the importance of accuracy [of form] from the beginning to the very end, he will have a sluggish habit of writing each character by itself. At some stage in the work it is necessary to place before the student the importance of letting go, of forcing the pace. . . .

The following excerpt [18:18, 19] contains an interesting picture of Gregg's activities in Chicago in 1899:

Next to the invention of the shorthand system itself, I
think the introduction and development of shorthand penmanship has given me the most satisfaction. At the National
Commercial Teachers Federation in 1899, I read a paper
entitled "Speed Practice," in which I advocated certain
theories that were then regarded as extremely radical and
preposterous, but that are today generally accepted as a
matter of course.

Among these theories was the training of students to write
fluently from the first lesson. I well remember how utterly
absurd that appeared to nearly all the teachers at the meeting,
because it was then an axiom that students should be taught
to "draw the characters slowly and carefully" until the theory
was mastered. . . .

I followed this demonstration with a series of shorthand
penmanship lessons in the *Gregg Writer,* the first attempt
of its kind. These lessons were afterwards reprinted in a
pamphlet form. They contained many useful suggestions;
but I am not proud of the shorthand in them, because they
were written late at night, at a time when I was personally
conducting a school day and evening, attending to my publishing business, preparing a revision of the *Shorthand
Manual,* editing the *Gregg Writer,* and writing almost everything in it, including the shorthand plates. But that pamphlet
started shorthand penmanship on its way.

The preceding excerpt gave 1899 as the date of Gregg's talk on
fluency at the beginning of the study of shorthand. The following
excerpt [6:274] would give a date of 1900 as the date of a similar
talk to the Eastern Commercial Teachers Association. Here Gregg
cautions his audience to remember that by "shorthand penmanship"
he is referring to fluency rather than to perfection of form. He warns
against insisting "too rigidly upon an absolutely perfect standard of
length, curvature, slant, etc."

Just thirty-nine years ago I gave an address before this
Association advocating the teaching of shorthand penmanship and outlining a series of simple drills for that purpose.
I believe that was the first time the expression "shorthand
penmanship" was used, and it certainly was the first time
the training of students to write the shorthand forms fluently
from the first lesson was advocated. It was then regarded
as a very radical idea, for at that time an accepted axiom
with teachers was that all through the theory work the
students should be trained to *"draw* the characters slowly
and carefully."

But here I want to say a word of caution. Like many good things, drills on shorthand penmanship may be, and often are, carried too far. Just as the old method of "drawing" the outlines, by establishing a sluggish habit of writing, proved an obstacle to rapid execution later, a rigid insistence on perfect outlines all through the theory work may be almost as detrimental. When a teacher insists too rigidly upon an absolutely perfect standard of length, curvature, slant, etc., he is likely to set up habits and inhibitions against fluency.

That talk from 1900 has not been preserved, but there is still in existence a copy of a talk [19:44] he gave in 1905 in which he repeats the same thought:

It is my opinion that in the past we have laid too great stress on *accuracy* and paid too little attention to the development of speed from a scientific point of view. It is a common fallacy that "speed will come with practice."

In the same volume [19:18], dated 1916, he said:

Do not expect too much precision of form at first; and above all things, avoid being hypercritical or "fussy." When the student has gained control of his shorthand and has a little more familiarity with the forms, you will have plenty of opportunity to enforce exactness of form, and your explanations will then be better understood and become more effective.

A summary of a convention talk by Gregg [4:14] gives so interesting a picture of the situation in 1930 that it is quoted rather fully. The discussion took place at the Iowa Research Conference on Commercial Education, Iowa City, in May, 1930. This summary was read, revised, and approved by Gregg before publication and correctly represents his views at that time.

In discussing the question of drop-outs in the shorthand department, Mr. Gregg talked very frankly. He stated that he began his career in shorthand by publishing statistics about the high percentage of failures in shorthand as a justification for a newer and better system, and he congratulated the teachers upon the improvement that had taken place. He said, among other things, that drop-outs are not confined to shorthand by any means, as all educational subjects are suffering from the restlessness of young people these days. But there are other causes.

One is the fact, known to everyone, that the commercial departments of high schools are being treated by many principals as a "dumping ground" for the mentally unfit or lazy students. Another is the fact that teachers of shorthand today, in the main, are not as competent as those thirty years ago. (Here there was a general gasp of surprise and protest.) Mr. Gregg went on to say that he acknowledged that teachers today had much better backgrounds educationally than formerly and were better trained in methods of teaching, but he maintained that they are not as skillful in the use of shorthand as they were thirty years ago.

He then mentioned the names of a great many teachers of thirty years ago who were able to go out and report any convention that came along. He said he doubted if there are many teachers who could do so today; in fact, he believes that if he called for a show of hands in any meeting of shorthand teachers of how many could write 100 words a minute for five minutes, there would not be many hands raised. And yet teachers of shorthand are handling a skill subject in which the best results can be obtained only by showing students the knack of doing the thing skillfully. Why this change?

Mr. Gregg said he believes it is due to the emphasis being placed in the wrong place. Teachers today are so busily engaged in researches (a general laugh), in surveys, in writing theses for degrees, that they have no time to learn how to write shorthand well, and, what is worse, the educational authorities do not care whether they do or not. Unless a teacher can write shorthand fluently and loves to write it and teach it, he cannot hope to inspire his students with love and enthusiasm for the art.

In this respect, at least, other countries are ahead of the United States, Mr. Gregg pointed out, and it is time we realized it. A teacher in Germany or Great Britain is not licensed to teach shorthand until he has demonstrated not merely his educational qualifications—his knowledge of teaching methods and class management and many other things—but is able to write rapidly for five minutes on difficult matter and transcribe it accurately. If we could establish such a standard for teachers of the subject in this country, it would do more to improve methods and results in shorthand than all the researches in the world, valuable as these are in giving a background and plan of work.

In closing this series of excerpts, we revert again to a matter that was especially dear to Gregg's heart—the idea that the learners should enjoy the learning of shorthand. This excerpt [6:277-278] occurs at the end of a talk he gave in 1939:

> Lastly, I urge you very strongly to establish the right attitude toward shorthand at the very outset. Many students come to the first lesson with the idea that shorthand is a dull, hard, uninteresting study. It is of the utmost importance that this idea should be banished from their minds as soon as possible. You and I know that shorthand is not only interesting but fascinating if it is taught in the right way. Try, then, to communicate your own interest and enthusiasm to your students, and it will make a vast difference in their work and, incidentally, in your own work. Why not take a few minutes at the beginning to tell them something about the history of shorthand, of the great people who have been writers of it—famous statesmen, such as Thomas Jefferson and Woodrow Wilson; great preachers, like John Wesley and his brother Charles, and Roger Williams, the founder of Rhode Island; four presidents of Harvard University; Dr. Timothy Dwight, president of Yale University; the famous Jonathan Edwards, first president of Princeton; famous authors, such as Charles Dickens, Arnold Bennett, Irvin Cobb, George Bernard Shaw, and many others; successful businessmen, such as George Cortelyou, John Raskob, William Loeb; and young people, like Swem, Dupraw, Schneider, and Anna Pollman, who have made shorthand a lever to advancement.
>
> Or you can place a simple outline like "make" on the blackboard and compare the number of strokes used in writing it to the great number of strokes required in longhand. You could also tell them that while studying shorthand they will be learning a great many other things, such as increasing their reading and writing vocabulary, and so on, and that if they never earn a dollar from the practice of shorthand they will have gained an invaluable accomplishment.
>
> That spirit of interest and enthusiasm, if established early, will help all through the course of study and will have a marvelous effect on the results secured.
>
> Recently I read a paragraph from a book by Professor Campagnac on *Education in Its Relation to the Common Purposes of Humanity,* in which this occurred: "A teacher, then, is a host who has invited the company of his pupils,

and their coming ought to be a pleasure and an honor to him. Not every teacher conveys this impression to his pupils; but not every teacher is a good teacher, and no teacher can be a good teacher unless he is truly a host to his pupils and shares with them what he has provided to celebrate their coming. I think there is no exception to this rule."

The two small volumes published by Gregg on methods of teaching have already been quoted in this part—*The Teaching of Shorthand* and *The Use of the Blackboard in Teaching Shorthand*. Purposely, however, very little of that material has been quoted, and the two books are presented here without changing or adding a word, although excisions have been made, to save space, of material that was timely when it was first published but that is no longer of general interest. Some of the talks from the early 1900's, for example, urged the teacher to compose his own graded connected material to supplement the very small amount that was then available in printed form. Such urgings are no longer pertinent in view of the wealth of graded connected material now available to every shorthand teacher. The three talks that follow are taken from the book *The Teaching of Shorthand*.

The Teaching of Shorthand: Some Suggestions to Young Teachers

IN teaching the theory of shorthand, as in teaching all other subjects, there are three main divisions:

1. THE PRESENTATION, or explanation of the lesson.

2. THE APPLICATION, or practice of the examples for the purpose of deepening the impression and developing skill.

3. THE EXAMINATION, or test for the purpose of ascertaining the results of the instruction and practice, and for the guidance of the teacher in assigning work.

These three processes are closely connected; and when properly applied, they result in knowledge, power, and skill. In each of these divisions you can apply an infinite variety of methods.

Let us consider these processes in the order I have given them.

THE PRESENTATION. A wide difference of views and methods exists in regard to presentation. Some teachers hold that the entire lesson should be explained in detail before the student is allowed to proceed with the study or practice of it; others maintain that no explanation should be given, as the student will have the principles more thoroughly impressed on his mind by working them out for himself and, in addition, will acquire self-reliance by so doing.

The great Pestalozzi says, "Never tell a child what he can find out for himself," and Herbert Spencer expresses the same thought, but not so sweepingly, when he says, "Students should be taught as little as possible and induced to discover as much as possible."

When Philip of Macedon presented his son, who afterwards became Alexander the Great, to Aristotle as a pupil, he said, "See that you make yourself useless to my son." A great teacher, using this expression as a text, has said: "Teach your pupils to think, show them the sources of information and teach them how to use those things with which they will have to do, and you have done more for them than you could possibly have done by cramming their minds with a thousand facts, useful though they may be."

But in connection with these wise maxims it should be borne in mind that the acquirement of shorthand involves not merely an intellectual understanding of rules and principles but actual *manual skill* in execution; therefore this theory of education should not be given too literal an application to shorthand instruction. Shorthand is *largely manual,* and the technique of execution can be most quickly secured by the imitation or practice of correctly written forms placed before the student as illustrations. For instance, when you place a shorthand form on the board, your students instinctively imitate your manner of writing and the actual form of the word or phrase.

Therefore between these extremes, of an exhaustive explanation of the lesson and no explanation whatever, I take the middle ground.

I believe that the teacher can best secure the attention and gain the confidence of the student by a brief but interesting and helpful explanation of the most important features of each lesson. I believe thoroughly in laying great emphasis on making the lessons *interesting.* Where you secure interest, you are bound to secure deep impression. Without the cheerful, magnetic influence of the teacher, there is always an atmosphere of discouragement in the shorthand classroom. A well-known teacher in discussing this subject said: "Some teachers make the mistake of requiring the student to dig his own way through the theory. Much valuable time is thus lost, and not a thing is gained. Interpret the author's text for the pupil, and get him to the main business of his course, *writing,* without a moment's delay."

There is no more helpful adjunct than a good blackboard. It is a pity that the value of blackboard work in teaching shorthand is not more fully realized. By the skillful use of the blackboard at all stages of shorthand study an energetic, resourceful teacher can most effectively arouse the interest and enthusiasm of the students, and secure satisfactory results. I most earnestly urge that you see to it that you have a good blackboard and the best chalk obtainable, and further that you practice assiduously to acquire a style of writing that will be an inspiration to your students.

• •

It may be asked, "What purpose is served by giving explanations and illustrations of rules so fully explained and illustrated in the textbook?" The chief purpose is to make a *vivid* impression on the memory of the student, who will remember the teacher's oral explanation and the blackboard illustrations long after the textbook rules and illustrations have faded from his memory. To quote from an address I made to teachers some years ago:

"I believe the teacher should be superior to the textbook, just as the finished actor rises above the written play. We read a play, and find it dull and lifeless; but when we see it interpreted by a great actor like Mansfield, it makes a vivid impression on our minds. So it is in teaching shorthand. Our pupils, being young, do not realize the necessity for careful preparation, and are likely to slight the lesson unless the teacher, by his personal force and the use of the blackboard, interests them in it."

• •

Cultivate simplicity of statement. The power of stating a thing in language so simple, clear, and direct as to be understood by the dullest student in the class is a great art.

In teaching, there is a temptation to elaborate, to be expansive. Train yourself to shun it relentlessly. A writer in one of the professional papers says:

Commercial teachers usually talk too much. They do too much for the student and communicate to him what he should get from his own observation and deliberation. A boy so trained will go into a business office and expect the proprietor to follow the same practice, but the proprietor does not do that, and consequently the boy is lost. A very important part of his training has been neglected. If I were to be asked what I consider the most important habit a teacher should cultivate, I should say, "Do not talk too much. Speak only when it is necessary. If you can, direct a student how to find out for himself what he requires. Give him a simple direction and let him do the rest himself." An enthusiastic teacher becomes so thoroughly saturated with his work that it is very natural for him to overdo the matter of instruction. From what I say it must not be inferred that I mean he should become so silent that he ceases to be an instructor. That is the other extreme. He should exercise a fine discriminating judgment in saying just the right word at the right time.

If a reader of this article, who is a teacher, will on the following day take himself in hand in the schoolroom and endeavor to condense into the fewest possible words the instruction he gives to his students, he will be astonished in a very short time at the great saving in his physical strength and the greater self-reliance and application which will shortly be observed in his students.

Now, brevity in speech must not be understood to mean surliness, curtness, or sarcasm. These are three weapons that come easy to the teacher, but which are boomerangs that return to the teacher and do far more harm than good. Sarcasm in the schoolroom is a splendid disciplinary agent, but it must be exercised with the utmost caution; curtness and surliness are never permissible.

No instruction is valuable which depends upon arbitrary practice or application without an understanding of the reason for the thing that is being applied. Therefore make it a practice to explain the *reason* for each rule or principle before the illustrations are practiced. With the fundamental rules, it is usually sufficient to explain that they represent the *natural way* of writing the forms.

• •

We come now to the second process—

THE APPLICATION. Having explained a rule clearly and briefly, direct the students to practice the illustrations which you have placed on the board.

• •

When you think it necessary, you may criticize and correct their outlines; but great tact should be exercised in doing this, especially during the first week or two. Find something to praise—the size of the characters, or some curve or joining, and then say, "But this form might be written a little better, like this——." An experienced teacher says: "Do not emphasize too strongly *criticisms* of pupils' errors. Do not overlook errors, but give more attention to, and say more in *commendation* of, what the student has done correctly. If the student is judiciously praised for everything that he writes correctly, the little that may be necessary to say about his errors is not likely to discourage him." *Praise first—criticize afterwards.*

Do not expect too much precision of form at first; and above all things avoid being hypercritical or "fussy." When the student has gained control of his hand and has a little more familiarity with the forms, you will have plenty of opportunity to enforce exactness of form, and your explanations will then be better understood and become more effective.

It often requires considerable self-control on the part of the teacher to refrain from interrupting students with many explanations and criticisms.

The student should clearly understand from the outset that shorthand is a study requiring much practice, and that he—not you—is to do that practice. *Start him right!* If you begin by explaining everything, correcting everything, giving him constant attention, he will expect you to continue to do so throughout the course, and will feel neglected and helpless when you are not at his elbow. Encourage him to acquire self-reliance, but let him know that you are always ready and willing to assist him when assistance is absolutely necessary.

• •

From motives of economy many schools supply students with cheap notebooks and pencils, and sometimes students buy such notebooks and pencils[1] at the stores. Nothing can be more detrimental to the progress of the shorthand student than poor materials. A well-known reporter says: "When I see some of the notebooks and pencils used by stenographers, I sometimes wonder how these stenographers manage to write. No mechanic could use poor tools in his work and produce good, fast work. Artists and experts are not satisfied with anything but the finest tools and instruments. The stenographer should have the same spirit. The cost of the best is only a trifle more, and the better and finer work done often results in a reduced size of writing which makes the best material the cheapest after all."

There is a lack of uniformity and orderliness in having various kinds of notebooks. Just as an orderly, well-kept office inspires the

---

[1] Ed. Note: In 1913 pencils were generally used for shorthand writing because of the unreliability of the pens of that time.

office force to be neat and orderly, so good notebooks and pencils inspire the student to do good work. Therefore see that your students have good notebooks and good pencils, and that they keep the pencils sharp, which will aid them in making neat, clean-cut outlines and insure a light touch.

Let us now consider the third process—

THE EXAMINATION. No part of the work is more important than tests and examinations to determine the student's knowledge of the principles of shorthand as he progresses, and perhaps no portion of the work is more neglected. It is in the examination that the intelligence, tact, industry, and teaching qualities of the teacher are brought out unmistakably. Show me a teacher's methods of testing students, grading papers, and system of promotion, and I will tell you the quality of his work—and the success he reaches in preparing stenographers for the exacting demands of modern business.

. . . .

A few comments on tests and examinations, as a whole, may be of service. There is a wide divergence of opinion as to the benefits of examinations. Some distinguished educators are opposed to examinations, but mainly on the ground that they interfere with continuous work; and for this reason I believe that the tests should be short, such as may be given in one period, so that they may not interfere with the onward progress of the student.

Properly conducted, examinations give students an opportunity to discover for themselves many of their weak points, and perhaps therein lies their greatest value. The examination is of much more benefit to the student than to the teacher. The teacher generally knows the student's capabilities. The examination serves also as a review, and brings all the work he has done into a comprehensive view, and is therefore of great value. The student should be induced to feel that the examination is but another form of recitation—that his actual knowledge of the subject is not affected by disclosing his weaknesses.

. . . .

In closing, let me say a word or two of the value of *personality* in getting results. A keen sympathy with the aims and ambitions of the students is one of the quickest means of getting into that close personal relationship which is so necessary for both student and teacher in the development of the student's abilities. This can best be attained by letting the student feel that you are a *leader* and *guide* and not a *critic*. Too many teachers, especially the younger and inexperienced, are apt to feel that they are not fulfilling their mission unless they put themselves in the attitude of critics. There can be no greater mistake. You at once antagonize the student, and all that confidence and freedom of expression, and that unfolding of his real self are lost to you—you never get at his better side, the side which will lead both him and you to success. If the student feels that you are his *guide and friend,* and that he can come to you in the fullest confidence, without fear of criticism, when he meets a difficult situation, you have done more for the development of that student than you could by all the criticisms you could ever make. On the other hand, there is such a thing as being too much of a guide—the student will *lean* on you instead of being self-reliant. The quality of self-reliance must be cultivated. He must learn that while you may plaster his pathway all along with signposts for his guidance, he must do the traveling for himself—that nothing can ever be substituted for his own energy, industry, intelligence, and initiative.

AN ADDRESS TO THE STUDENTS IN THE SUMMER
NORMAL SCHOOL FOR SHORTHAND TEACHERS,
GREGG SCHOOL, CHICAGO
[*Probably 1913*]

The Art of Teaching Shorthand

• •

AS the business man of today has been educated to demand a higher standard of efficiency in his stenographic force than formerly, there must be a corresponding advance in the methods of teaching shorthand and typewriting if we would meet these requirements. The demand for speed in execution has grown in the profession of shorthand as in everything else. Work of all kinds is now done under greater pressure than ever before.

The keen competition between commercial schools seems to render it impracticable to lengthen the course of instruction materially, and yet the teacher of today is expected to produce *much better equipped* stenographers and typewriter operators than formerly, not only from the standpoint of technical skill, but of a wider cultural education. This additional cultural work can be done effectively in the high school by the lengthening of the course, but the commercial school must produce results in a shorter time. It is necessary, therefore, for the teacher in the commercial school to intensify his instruction. While it is safe to say that the time devoted to the subjects included in a shorthand course has not been increased to any appreciable extent in the business school, there has been in the past ten years a demand by business men of fully twenty-five per cent increase in efficiency, which means that the students must accomplish just that much more in the time that custom has established as necessary to prepare for stenographic work.

This being the case, it is obvious that improved methods of instruction are imperatively demanded to meet present-day conditions.

And while this demand for increased efficiency has been growing and is still growing at a tremendous rate, there can be no change in the fundamental processes of writing shorthand—processes that are entirely distinct from any improvement in the shorthand systems themselves—and must ever be present, whatever the shorthand system used. Let us consider briefly what these processes are, and we shall realize how great are the problems involved in teaching shorthand, as well as in acquiring sufficient skill in writing to meet existing requirements. A keen analytical writer on this subject has said:

There are at least five distinct mental operations carried on continuously during verbatim reporting. First, there is the sensation of sound received by the ear. Second, there is the perception by the brain of the word uttered—practically simultaneously with the sensation of hearing in the case of a distinct speaker, but often delayed a large fraction of a second when a speaker drops his voice, or a witness in court has a foreign accent. In the third place, the stenographer must analyze the structure of all the less common words in the sentences, all except the stock words or phrases, which he writes by a practically automatic habit. Fourth, these relatively uncommon words must be put on paper according to the principles of the system employed. This one operation involves many subordinate and infinitely swift efforts of recollection, association, and decision. Fifth, all these mental operations are carried on while the pen or pencil is from two or three words to an entire sentence behind the speaker—this of course in rapid speaking —thereby complicating the situation by compelling memory to keep pace with attention. In other words, while the scribe is writing the predicate of one sentence and analyzing an unfamiliar word in the subject of the next, he is at the same time giving his auditory attention to the predicate of the second sentence then being uttered by the speaker. This is impossible to an untrained mind. The average educated person cannot retain more than perhaps six or eight words of the exact phraseology of a speaker at one time. The competent stenographer can hold ten, fifteen, twenty words, or even more in his memory, while at the same time taxing his mind by the act of writing the words that preceded.

The truth of what this writer says is obvious to us all and there is forced upon us at once the conclusion that the teaching of shorthand presents some peculiar and distinctive problems in pedagogy. I say "peculiar and distinctive" because the ordinary principles of pedagogy cannot always be applied in shorthand instruction, because it is an entirely distinctive problem.

The teaching of bookkeeping is largely a mental problem; the teaching of penmanship is largely a manual one. The teaching of shorthand combines both problems—and in a combination that is complex in the highest degree.

In teaching bookkeeping it is not of great importance that the work be done quickly. Speed here, as elsewhere, is desirable; but it *is* of the greatest importance that it be done *accurately*. One of our problems is the thorough correlation of these two phases of shorthand work—that is, of acquiring *both* speed and accuracy.

Let me draw your attention for a moment to the last-named condition of which the writer just quoted speaks, namely—the training of the memory, and the development of concentration, to enable the student to remember as many words as possible while recording other words. Memory training and complete concentration, to my mind, present a distinctive factor in the teaching of shorthand—memorizing not in the sense of storing up in the mind facts or information for future use, but temporarily holding suspended the exact words of a speaker, given perhaps very rapidly, until they can be written, to be then forgotten.

This training must necessarily be a part of the course in the training of all shorthand students and, until the ability to retain a large number of words is developed, a high degree of skill cannot be attained;

and this factor, as has been said before, is quite distinct from the *mastery of the principles* of shorthand, and is not affected by the *system* which is being studied. It is this faculty that gives the expert shorthand writer the ability to make the process of writing *continuous*. It *may* be possible to simplify the principles of shorthand construction, so that the mind may construct the word forms more easily, and it *may* be possible to render the joinings and characters more easy and natural, so as to lessen the manual labor in executing them, as has been done in modern systems, but it is not possible in a few hours to endow the student with the trained memory which will permit of the performance of the complex mental and manual acts required in very rapid shorthand writing.

• • • • • • • • • • • • • • • • • • • •

Let us return to the acts involved in shorthand writing—for I have not mentioned all of them. While the writer of shorthand is hearing, thinking out, remembering, and recording the words of the speaker or dictator, he has other work to do. He must turn the pages of his notebook from time to time, make corrections occasionally, observe proportion in writing the characters—all operations necessitating a share of the attention. If he is to make an intelligent report, he must pay close attention to the purport of the speaker's remarks. This last phase of the work is of the highest importance in making an intelligent transcript, being almost impossible if the writer is unable to comprehend the meaning of what the speaker is saying.

It has been said that the practice of shorthand brings into active, instantaneous operation all the faculties of the mind, and that the attainment of a high degree of skill in shorthand writing is equivalent to a proportionate increase in mental activity.

From this partial statement of what is done in actual shorthand writing, it will be clear that the teaching of the subject has distinctive problems and affords the teacher exceptional opportunities for diversified methods.

How shall we develop speed with accuracy in the shortest possible time? In other words, how shall we prepare our students to become efficient stenographers and at the same time give them that correct fundamental training which shall enable them to develop a high degree of skill?

It is my opinion that in the past we have laid too great stress upon *accuracy* and paid too little attention to the development of speed from a scientific point of view. It is a common fallacy that "speed will come with practice."

Without in the least depreciating the importance of accuracy, I believe that we have insisted too much upon accuracy without regard to speed, and by so doing have fastened upon our students a sluggish method of forming the characters from which, in many cases, they have been unable to free themselves in after years. I am firmly of the belief that *speed in execution should be developed along with a theoretical knowledge of the principles, and not postponed until the writer has mastered the principles.*

I have heard teachers, in speaking about this matter, say, "Oh, well, the students will learn the knack of speed in actual work outside the school." That view of the matter is a survival of the old idea, now fast dying out. Accuracy and speed can be combined from the very beginning, and should be. Who can say that the steps of a runner are any less accurate than are those of the walker? The secret of speed in execution lies largely in getting the right idea.

•   •   •   •   •   •   •   •   •   •   •   •   •   •   •   •   •   •   •

We can't get away from the fact that rapid shorthand writing is largely a matter of *manual* skill. Shorthand writing is *writing,* not drawing. This fact must become a fixture in the mind of the student from the first day of his work, and it must be doubly impressed that all that is written must be read. I am not one who believes that the shorthand characters must be drawn with mathematical accuracy in the early lessons. I think the characters must be correct, and held as nearly as possible to the ideal, but they must be *written* so, not drawn.

Many teachers are a little too "textbooky," if I may so express it. They use modern textbooks written from the teacher's point of view; they know these books from cover to cover, and they teach the principles much more thoroughly than the teacher of the old school; but when they have done all that, they are apt to think that the development of speed lies entirely with the student, and that all he needs is continuous dictation practice. They feel that they have done their part in teaching rules and form, and the rest lies with the student and his employer.

•   •   •   •   •   •   •   •   •   •   •   •   •   •   •   •   •   •   •

One of the most powerful aids in imparting to others the knack of writing shorthand *rapidly* is the ability to write rapidly and to demonstrate how it is done. Not rapidity in the sense that the teacher must be a "record breaker," or a "speedist," but he ought to have sufficient executional skill to show students that he is a capable writer himself. And it may be remarked in passing that the teacher who takes the trouble to acquire this skill will have revealed to him some of the things behind the scenes which will do more to help him to secure results than anything he has ever undertaken.

It is not sufficient to give general suggestions from time to time, for such academic instruction, however valuable it may be, leaves only a transient impression on the mind of the average student and is of little practical value in the development of speed.

To be of any effective service, the instruction must be supplemented by regular and intense application under the eye of the teacher.

READ BEFORE THE CENTRAL COMMERCIAL TEACHERS' ASSOCIATION, OMAHA, NEBRASKA, MAY, 1905
[*This talk was given at a time when very few high schools taught shorthand.*]

"Tricks of the Trade" in Teaching Shorthand

THE title of my paper was suggested by the concluding remark of a school proprietor who applied to me for a teacher. After mentioning the requirements, he said: "To sum it all up, I want a man who is thoroughly qualified—one who knows all the tricks of the trade." At first, I was inclined to resent the imputation that there were any tricks in our trade, but subsequent reflection and observation have convinced me that we cannot, with truth, say "there are tricks in all trades but ours."

WHAT "TRICKS OF THE TRADE" MEANS. The phrase is not used in a derogatory sense; in our profession it is usually intended to convey the idea of adaptability, tact, experience, etc. In every line of human endeavor, the man who is valuable to his employer is the man who knows the tricks of his trade. It is just as true in our profession as it is of the shoe clerk who sells you a pair of shoes for seven dollars when you intended to purchase a pair for half that amount on entering the store. And by that it is not meant the man who is familiar with all the sharp practices and underhanded tricks of a trade, but the man who makes friends because of his knowledge of his business and of human nature, and who, by his industry, foresight, and adaptability to different personalities, is able to make the best use of his knowledge. Such is the man who is familiar with the legitimate "tricks" of his trade. It is he who reaches the highest success in any line, whose force is felt not only in his own particular profession, but carries the influence of his forcefulness into all branches of human activity. But, back of this familiarity with human nature, there must be a wider and deeper knowledge—knowledge of the thousands of details, small in themselves, but which go to make up the whole.

• • • • • • • • • • • • • • • • • • • •

MASTERY OF THE SUBJECTS.   First of all, it goes without saying, he should be master of the theory and technique of the art which he teaches. This is an indispensable trick. Nothing carries conviction so quickly or is the source of greater inspiration to his students than evidence that the teacher can do what he teaches.

The teacher who gives a practical demonstration of his ability to perform the feats which he asks of his pupils, has done more perhaps to gain the confidence of his students than he could by any other means. There is such a wide difference between the theory of any art and the application of the theory to practical work that it seems to me this is a point that should receive a great deal of earnest attention from the teacher. Methods of execution in writing can only be taught by practical illustration. One may have an almost perfect conception of how a thing should be done, and yet not be able to do it until he has seen it done. Such knowledge does not come from a mere conception that this or that thing can be done; it comes only after infinitely patient toil.

But, in illustrating a point, the teacher should not allow his own expertness in execution to become so apparent as to discourage his students. He should endeavor to keep his execution within the bounds of the capacity of his students; it should be an illustration of the methods of movements rather than a demonstration of the speed at which such movements may be made, otherwise the effect may be opposite from that which he desires. If he can create the impression upon the students that it is all very simple, and that by a little extra effort they can do as well, he will unconsciously develop in them a feeling of power that will have the most beneficial effect.

•   •   •   •   •   •   •   •   •   •   •   •   •   •   •   •   •   •   •

PERSONAL INTEREST IN STUDENTS.   A very important point is for the teacher to take a personal interest in the progress of each student, but this must be done without creating any suspicion of partiality. Only by a constant study of the peculiarities of each student, in order that he may give him such encouragement as he needs and point out tactfully the errors of his ways in such a manner as not to antagonize him, can the teacher hope to attain this end. The element of personal interest in his students is a potent one in influencing the success of the teacher as well as that of the student. It is a "trick" that can be acquired only by painstaking care, and requires the exercise of rare discrimination, self-control, and a strong sense of justice. It is an art that should be cultivated assiduously. The school proprietor can get students to the school. The success of the student is then practically in the teacher's hands, and the fitness of the teacher for the position which he holds will depend upon how well the pupil accomplishes his task. The teacher should bring every influence to bear to make the progress of the student so sure and thorough that when he leaves, whether it be in six months or a year, he will be qualified to discharge his duties creditably to himself and to the institution where he received his training. While the teacher is employed primarily to "teach," there is much more to be taught than the mere art of shorthand writing. He should make a study of the defects in the training of his students, and try as far as possible to correct them. Anything that would tend to lessen the student's chances for success, such as lack of taste in dress, untidiness, peculiar mannerisms, etc., may be corrected by occasional general talks on such subjects, and in extreme cases by tactful confidential talks. It is manifestly impossible for teachers handling large classes to remember the name of each student at all times—although it will be surprising to those who have not tried it how quickly the faculty can be acquired—but it is a habit that the teacher should acquire as early in his experience as possible. There is hardly anything more displeasing to the student than for his teacher to neglect to address him by name.

SECURING THE ATTENTION OF STUDENTS.   The art of holding the attention of the student while presenting the lesson; of repeating the explanations, if need be, in different language, until they have been thoroughly impressed on the mind of the student, is a subject that will require much earnest study on the part of the teacher.

At this point the teacher will have full opportunity to exercise whatever ingenuity and resourcefulness he may possess, because methods of presentation that would appeal quickly and effectively to one class of students, might have exactly the opposite effect on others. The teacher should make a careful study of the personnel of his classes, and adopt methods that will comprehend the various mental capabilities of his students, if possible. A mistake many inexperienced teachers make is to adapt their methods to a few of the bright pupils of one class, to the utter confusion of the less intellectual students.

•   •   •   •   •   •   •   •   •   •   •   •   •   •   •   •   •   •

THE USE OF THE BLACKBOARD.   Perhaps nothing marks the difference between the experienced teacher and the novice more than the method of using the blackboard, and I would name the intelligent use of the blackboard as one of the greatest tricks in our trade. From the position that he assumes before the board, the inexperienced teacher often appears to believe that his pupils can see through him, I mean in the literal sense. But in our profession the art of "side-stepping" is just as important as it is in the noble art of self-defense. The experienced teacher after writing the outlines on the board will step aside in an easy, natural manner so that students in all parts of the room may have a clear view of the board. The young teacher is very apt to write his outlines so small and faint that they cannot be seen by any except those who are close at hand. The knack of retaining proportion of outline while writing large on the board is a trick that requires considerable practice.

KEEPING "JUST AHEAD" OF STUDENTS.   The inexperienced teacher is frequently inclined to "show off" by writing very rapidly on the board, to the utter bewilderment of his students. This may impress them with a due appreciation of his ability as a writer of shorthand, but it has a most discouraging effect on the student who contrasts his snail-like execution with that of the teacher. On the other hand, the teacher who has, through long training and experience, mastered the method of handling blackboard work, will write just a little ahead of his pupils—enough to make them feel that with a little effort they could do as well—but he will always be *just ahead* of his pupils.

GENIALITY—AND DISCIPLINE.   The teacher should possess a genial and amiable disposition, but he should not allow the discipline of his room to become lax in his efforts to be good natured, nor should he allow students to get the idea that the acquisition of a business education is anything but a serious matter. He should glow with such a warmth of good-will as to be a constant incentive to his students to emulate his example. He must put vim and enthusiasm into his work; all his acts must be so businesslike that his students will unconsciously acquire the habit. He must cultivate his memory so that he will be relentless in getting the work he requires of his students. He should be very careful, however, in deciding upon a policy, to be sure that he can carry it out. Work started by a teacher, and afterwards abandoned, will create a feeling of distrust in his ability.

A moderate amount of work thoroughly accomplished each day will be far more effective than a large amount imperfectly gone over. Students are very quick to detect imperfections in a teacher's character, and weak points in his methods, and he must therefore constantly strive to make his work as strong as possible. The teacher should impress upon his pupils the advantage of thorough preparation, and show them the folly of leaving school before they are competent to fill the best positions. I believe that the teacher in advocating a long course is rendering the student the greatest possible service, as well as doing his full duty by his employers and to the commercial community. Business men nowadays make such exacting requirements of stenographers that it is imperative that the school expecting to keep in the front rank should so qualify its students that they can enter upon their duties without having to go through a long course of "breaking in."

It will require rare judgment on the part of the teacher to effect this result without creating the suspicion that he is working solely for his employer's interests.

KEEPING UP TO DATE. The wide-awake teacher will keep fully alive to the methods pursued by business houses in the handling of correspondence. Methods change constantly, and the teacher who would attain the greatest success, and enlarge his influence in his profession, must keep up to date in his methods. He can do this by keeping in close touch with his former students who have gone out into the business world, and by reading the shorthand magazines. And while he is making a study of these methods, he should not forget the hundreds of ambitious teachers who, perhaps, may not be so fortunately situated for studying methods, and give them the benefit of his experience through this Association and the shorthand magazines.

DIFFERENCES IN SCHOOL CONDITIONS. It has often occurred to me that in all the meetings of this Association which I have attended there has never been any reference made to the differences existing between the methods of conducting a day school and a night school in a large city. These are important considerations, and personally I should like to hear them discussed. When I visit a school in a small town, I always envy the shorthand teacher the class of students he has under his charge. They are generally earnest and ambitious and are willing to devote considerable time to practice outside school hours. The city student, as a rule, is not so thorough in his work, and it is a severe drain upon the teacher's energies to keep him sufficiently interested to perform the work assigned to him.

DAY SCHOOL AND NIGHT SCHOOL. The same difference exists between the day school and the night school in a large city. In the day school the students are usually very young; and as they have no idea of the value of time, it is imperative that the teacher should be constantly on the alert. In the night school the students are older; and as they are employed during the day, they are accustomed to strict discipline and continuous labor. As they have taken up the study of choice, and have not been sent by their parents, they are liable to discontinue the study at any time unless they are kept interested and believe they are making satisfactory progress.

Night school work has always had a fascination for me, perhaps because of my desire to help those who are trying to help themselves. I believe that the methods employed in the night school should differ materially from those of the day school. As the night school students are employed in the business hours, they know a great deal about office routine, business terms and forms, and consequently they require less instruction in these things. They can apply their shorthand and typewriting more readily on that account; but as they are at work all day, it is absolutely essential that they should be kept interested and wide-awake. Less copying work should therefore be assigned to them, and they should be given a great deal more blackboard and dictation work. As they have already acquired businesslike habits of deportment, the teacher can assume toward them a more genial attitude than is possible in the day school. This adaptability to the varying needs of the day and night school is one of the tricks I would require above all others in a teacher in my employ.

•   •   •   •   •   •   •   •   •   •   •   •   •   •   •   •   •   •   •

IMPORTANCE OF WELL-DIRECTED ENERGY. In closing I desire to mention that which in any line of business counts for more, perhaps, with one exception—brains—than any other, and that is, well-directed energy. To a teacher, energy is as indispensable as a mastery of the subject he teaches. A teacher using mediocre or even inferior methods, who backs up his work with snap and energy, will accomplish creditable results where a more brilliant man with less energy would prove a failure. The successful teacher must be able to create an atmosphere of energetic action that will arouse his pupils to put forth their best efforts. But he must learn to judge between apparent energy and actual energy. Nothing is more absurd than a man rushing hither and thither, sputtering and fuming, in the belief that he is accomplishing something. It is the escaping steam that makes the noise. A teacher may possess a vast storehouse of energy and yet fail to accomplish results because of his inability to direct his energy in the proper channels.

The teacher must be the adviser and guardian spirit of his pupil; and it should be his constant care to see that each day marks a distinct step on life's road, and that, above all, the student can never say, "I came out by the same door wherein I entered."

READ BEFORE THE NATIONAL SHORTHAND TEACHERS' ASSOCIATION, ST. LOUIS, MISSOURI, 1901
[*This was an association of business school teachers.*]

The Use of the Blackboard in Teaching Shorthand

TEACHING THROUGH THE EYE. *Hardly any other subject in teaching lends itself so well to blackboard illustration as does shorthand. Shorthand is essentially *writing,* and the blackboard is the ideal medium for conveying to a number of students the ideas you wish to express. You can teach them more in a few well-executed outlines on the board than you can by many minutes of talking, for there is much truth in the old saying that "seeing is believing."

The average class of shorthand pupils is made up of three learning types—those who learn mainly through their eyes, those who acquire knowledge chiefly through their ears, and those who depend upon both eyes and ears. By far the greatest number learn through their eyes.

Blackboard illustration, being intensely graphic, focuses attention and impresses forms and principles so vividly that the student carries them away with him permanently. •Textbook illustrations go much farther in real teaching than any amount of printed description. But they cannot go so far as the teacher goes in his illustrations on the board. The teacher can demonstrate movement, which is just as important as form, because form is the result of movement. This the textbook illustration cannot give. '

Any teacher who is thoroughly versed in his art knows, however, that there are forms for words, combinations, and phrases that have to be *shown,* if they are to be assimilated; and he must realize that the time saved in "showing" an entire class at one time is infinitely precious. The blackboard becomes the illuminating center. ·With its) aid the teacher can appeal to the eyes of all his students at one time, showing them not only the correct outlines to write, but also the correct, the easiest, the expert way to write them. Those blackboard outlines are going to make an impression.• Seen with the eyes, they are going to be photographed on the brain, and from the brain transmitted to the hand.

•   •

I have always had a profound belief in the educational advantage of good blackboard work in the shorthand classroom. When a fine specimen of shorthand is seen on the blackboard, seldom indeed does one find the notes of the students awkward and sprawling.•A teacher who takes a pride in the attainment of an excellent style of shorthand is not likely to be satisfied to have students write poor shorthand; and as the students are interested in the shorthand written by their teacher, the forms on the blackboard make an indelible impression upon their minds.

•Shorthand is largely manual, and the technique of execution can be most quickly secured by the imitation or practice of correctly written forms placed before the student as illustrations. When a teacher places a shorthand form on the board, the students instinctively imitate the manner of writing and the actual form of the word or phrase, so that they are started off on the right road at once. They set out on the road to high speeds, high position, and high salary—the Shorthand High Road, in fact—with a full and perfect equipment of correct ideas and correct *ideals* which combine the art of fine penmanship with accurate, legible shorthand.

There is, therefore, a great responsibility resting on the teacher to practice assiduously to acquire a style of blackboard writing that will be a constant inspiration to his students.

Dread of the board: There are teachers who regard the blackboard with dread not unmixed with scorn. They dread the "ordeal" of the writing itself, because they are conscious of a lack of skill in execution and have a fear of making mistakes. Therefore they are inclined to look with disfavor on the blackboard as an aid to instruction. But the teacher who fears making mistakes will not get very far in the teaching profession. The human element is always present and there is no such thing as perfection. A very little time spent in practice will bring an easy, accurate style which will add both to his teaching ability and to his standing with his classes.

A school manager once said to me: "I am not quite satisfied with the work of Miss A. She does not get results that are equal to those of Miss L last year."

Then he added: "I don't know shorthand—wish I did—but I notice that our former teacher used the blackboard a great deal in drilling the students and that Miss A never makes use of it. I have wondered if it is because she is not a good writer and does not know the system thoroughly. It seems to me that shorthand must be like penmanship and that good examples on the blackboard help to encourage and inspire the students. They will imitate what they see on the board; and, if it is good, it will help them wonderfully. Anyway, it makes a strong visual impression, which should be helpful, assuming, of course, that the teacher has a good style of writing."

I agreed with him. Then he went on:

"That shorthand classroom of ours is lifeless this year, and I want a teacher next year who can use the blackboard as Miss L did and wake 'em up."

THE ART OF BLACKBOARD DEMONSTRATION. And now a word as to the art itself—for blackboard demonstration *is* an art in itself.

It will be obvious that Gregg Shorthand lends itself particularly well to artistic blackboard demonstration. And, as artistry means speed

—since graceful curves could never be made haltingly or clumsily—
it is well worth the shorthand teacher's while to take pains in making
his blackboard writing as pleasing as possible.

•   •

Special points of technique: But what is to constitute the teacher's
own practice? How is he to acquire that fluent perfect style, those
artistic outlines, and that general proficiency at the blackboard?

The most important point is that the teacher should be *interested*
in blackboard work. If he looks upon it as a "got-to-be-done" task, it
will show signs of his grudging labors.

He can make it interesting—interesting to himself—by treating it as
a subject in itself, to be studied just as any other subject is studied.
He should delve into its possibilities and its value. He should aim at
a high standard of neatness and excellence, and practice assiduously
to attain the standard that he sets.

Handling the chalk: Among the points which the teacher will find
worthy of special care and special attention is the method of handling
the chalk.

Many teachers grip the chalk too tightly, just as the beginner in
golf grips his clubs with rigid muscles until he has learned the knack
of the game. The chalk should be held lightly, and should be turned
from time to time as the writing proceeds. Changing its position slightly
prevents the wear from coming all in one place and so aids in making
forms of uniform thickness of line.

It is of the utmost importance that the chalk be held correctly.
The mode of holding is different from that of holding a pen or pencil.
It should be held at a greater slant than is adopted in holding a pencil,
and the end of the chalk should point towards the palm of the hand.
A new piece of chalk should be broken in two and the broken end
of one portion should be applied to the board.

In night school classes teachers have found that yellow, medium-
soft chalk can be seen more plainly and is easier on the eyes than
is white chalk.

Position at the board: A common fault is that of standing too
close to the board. When the writer is too close to the board, it is
impossible to give a free, vigorous, graceful swing to the writing; nor
can one get the correct visual impression of the forms. The latter is
of great importance. Without a clear visual impression it is impossible
to preserve lineality, slant, curvature, proportion, etc.

The correct position is nearly an arm's length from the board. The eraser should be held in the left hand, preferably behind the back. Wherever practicable the outlines should be written above the head so that all the pupils may see easily the movement of the teacher's arm as he executes the word form, "for the *act* is worth just as much to the learner as the *result,* and sometimes more."

Lack of lineality: When the writing slants downwards or upwards at the end of the line of writing, it shows that the writer has not a correct visual impression of what he is doing. In some cases this is due to incorrect position, but in most cases to the fact that the writer does not move along as he writes. In other words, the teacher assumes a position at the beginning of the line, and as the writing proceeds he remains in that position, merely stretching out his arm to form the characters at the end of the line. This practice inevitably results in a lack of lineality.

• •

"Side-stepping" in board work: When the writing is finished, the teacher should always step far enough away from the board to permit *all* students to have an unobstructed view of *all the writing* on the board. Students who are seated in the left-hand corner of the room very often suffer from the forgetfulness of teachers in this matter.

The blackboard should never be placed at the side of the room near one corner or end, for then some pupils will have to view it at such an acute angle as to disort seriously the proportion, shape, and slant of the forms.

The outlines themselves should be just large enough to be readily visible from any point in the room. All the strokes should be vivid and clear without sacrificing the characteristic lightness. The lines should be bright and sharp—not dull, gray, lifeless.

As a rule, that picture is best which looks best at a distance. So, too, as a rule, that blackboard writing is best which looks best at the back of the room. It is well, ~~therefore,~~ for the teacher to make sure of the visibility of his outlines by walking to various points of the room after each writing, and by studying the effect of the copy upon himself. He may find, for instance, that, while the outlines are correct in size and are vivid, yet a strong light is shining from above the blackboard directly into the eyes of the pupils, making the outlines almost invisible to them.

• •

"Raggedness": Students should be taught to acquire the swift, facile way of commencing and finishing each outline as it should be commenced and finished, without superfluous "ends" or flicks of the pen and gaps where gaps should not be.

A board adorned with outlines that are perfect in these particulars, as in every other, will show the students that the little extra care needed will be well spent, and that the *art* of shorthand writing means speed, accuracy—and satisfaction.

Telling them that shorthand is an art won't convince them. They know shorthand as a useful, practical subject, but one doesn't associate *art* with a useful, practical science. Art is—oh, something airy, dreamy, impractical. How can *art* be mentioned in the same breath with businesslike, practical shorthand! More work for the blackboard!

Show them: Well, it's the teacher's job to make those students understand and believe that shorthand is something in which both hand and eye can delight—an art to be loved for itself, and not simply as a means to an end. And the teacher can make them understand these things only by showing them—by showing them artistic writing, not just once, but all the time, so that they will come to *think* artistic shorthand and to *write* artistic shorthand, which means legible, easy, and swift shorthand.

The things which count: Judgment in the matter of spacing and even proportion of outlines, scrupulous care of the blackboard itself, and sufficient zest are the most important factors in the training— "self" or otherwise—of a good blackboard writer.

Self-consciousness, always a drawback to the teacher, is more than ever a drawback when it comes to blackboard work. Self-consciousness begets a rigid, unnatural pose—fatal to beauty in shorthand outlines. It is necessary for the teacher to train until he loses himself in his zest for blackboard writing, for in that way only will he gain those relaxed arm and body movements without which graceful writing cannot be.

Theory knowledge—sureness of all the principles—goes hand in hand with writing practice on the board. The slightest hesitation over a knotty point in theory will cause an outline to "hesitate" in sympathy, and then beauty and flow will both be sacrificed.

Beauty of outline, however, should always be the teacher's chief objective. It is all inclusive, embracing a thorough knowledge of the theory. It is the reward of unselfish, persistent study and practice at the blackboard. With it the teacher has one of the most powerful teaching aids known to psychology. The continuous appeal, through the student's eye, to his love of the beautiful awakens into vigorous activity a retentive memory, so that the resulting strong kinesthetic images induce the desired response from the student's fingers. His notebook is as a mirror, reflecting in all their beauty the artistic outlines placed on the blackboard by his teacher.

•   •

THEORY DEMONSTRATION. We had occasion recently to visit a schoolroom which had blackboards on four walls, and each of them was filled with beautifully written shorthand. Some of the outlines were to illustrate principles that were being explained, but the orderliness and the artistic quality of all the shorthand commanded our profound admiration.

The teacher in this school, it is needless to say, gets splendid results. An examination of the notes of the students showed that they all reflected with remarkable fidelity the quality of the notes on the board. It is very natural that they should, because the learning of "style" in shorthand is largely a matter of imitation, and the characteristics of the teacher's blackboard notes will be copied almost unconsciously by the students. To thoughtful teachers there is a tremendous educational significance in this fact.

We had in our Chicago school a few years ago two teachers between whom there sprang up an intense rivalry in the matter of artistic shorthand. Beauty of outlines and technical skill became a hobby with them. Their enthusiasm was communicated to the students as well as to the other teachers; and as a result, the quality of the shorthand notes in the whole school was raised to a very high standard.

There is a "practical" side to the question, too. We all appreciate the importance of accurate notes and good penmanship as factors in *legibility*. Good notes are the result of correct ideals and the right sort of practice while the principles are being learned. Artistic blackboard notes give the correct ideal and deepen impression.

•   •

Confidence can be stimulated, too, by a little healthy encouragement from the teacher in the way of public praise of those outlines that are conspicuously good. The condemnation of mistakes in public is always a pedagogic blunder, but a little praise where praise is due— or even *almost* due!—can work wonders, particularly with the beginner.

•   •

Some pitfalls to avoid: There are rocks in the pathway to blackboard perfection—rocks over which the ordinary teacher may stumble. They are those little blunders of style that seem to mean so little, but really mean so much.

Sheer nervousness—fear of the sound of their own voices—makes some teachers mumble their comments while still facing towards the board. Even teachers who are not nervous have this disastrous habit. It *is* disastrous, because when the students hear a confused murmuring through the back of the teacher's head, but cannot make out one single syllable of the words he is uttering, they will be more than tempted to treat his teachings with a half-amused tolerance. They will certainly lose interest; and then dignity and authority will totter, and the beneficial training that might have been derived from the demonstration will be lost forever.

It is a mistake to talk at all while actually writing on the board. It is far better to finish; then turn and state clearly the brief facts about the prominent points in the lesson.

It is a mistake, too, to display shorthand errors on the board. Errors seen will be retained by the mind and are apt to become confused with the correct forms.

"Showing off": The temptation to "show off" constitutes another stumbling block—with young teachers in particular. The teacher should beware of adopting a fussy, time-wasting method of approaching the board, with much preliminary circling of the arm and unnecessary movement at the end of each stroke. This, with affectation and wordiness in the verbal presentation of the lesson, does more harm than good, for it alienates interest and courts ridicule. Students assimilate the affectation with the instruction and, because they are young, it remains with them, hampering them later in their speed work.

There are teachers who fall into the error of forgetting the importance of the students' "seeing how it is done," which is the main object of blackboard demonstrating. It is a mistake to have matter ready on the board when the class assembles. The students do not know how slowly or how carefully those good-looking characters were made. They may even suspect the use of a key. They derive far more benefit from watching the actual, facile, graceful writing itself. "Ready-made" blackboard copy is ordinary, dull, conventional—dead. The watching of actual work on the board is something "live" and full of interest.

Keeping "just ahead" of students: The inexperienced teacher is frequently inclined to "show off" by writing very rapidly on the board, to the utter bewilderment of his students. This may duly impress them with his ability as a writer of shorthand, but it has a most discouraging effect on the student who contrasts his snail-like execution with that of the teacher.

In illustrating a point, the teacher should endeavor to keep his execution within the bounds of the capacity of his students—it should be an illustration of the methods of movements rather than of the speed at which such movements may be made; otherwise the effect may be opposite from that which he desires. If he can create the impression upon the students that the process is all very simple, and that by a little extra effort they can do as well, he will unconsciously develop in them a feeling of power that will have the most beneficial effect.

Sources of Quotations in Part 4

1. Gregg, John Robert. *Basic Principles of Gregg Shorthand.* New York, The Gregg Publishing Company, 1923.

2. ————. "The Development of Shorthand Speed," *Second Yearbook*, Eastern Gregg Shorthand Teachers Association, 1915.

3. ————. "Discussion," *Second Yearbook*, Gregg Shorthand Association of America. (Second Annual Convention, Peoria, Illinois, July, 1902)

4. ————. "Discussion of Teacher Training," *The American Shorthand Teacher* (September, 1930), p. 14.

5. ————. "The Evolution of Gregg Shorthand," *The Gregg Writer*, XXXIII (June, 1931), pp. 455-458, 480.

6. ————. "Improvement of Classroom Teaching in Shorthand," *Twelfth Yearbook*, Eastern Commercial Teachers Association, 1939.

7. ————. *Gregg Shorthand, Revised Edition*, Chicago, The Gregg Publishing Company, 1902.

8. ————. *Gregg Shorthand, New and Revised Edition.* New York, The Gregg Publishing Company, 1916.

9. ————. *Gregg Shorthand, Anniversary Edition*, New York, The Gregg Publishing Company, 1929.

10. ————. *Gregg's Shorthand, Revised Edition.* Stratford-on-Avon, England, The Gregg Publishing Company, 1901.

11. ————. *Gregg Speed Studies.* New York, The Gregg Publishing Company, 1917.

12. ————. "Kitty Dixon Taylor—A Tribute," *The Business Education World*, XXI (March, 1941), pp. 603-604.

13. ————. *Light-Line Phonography—The Phonetic Handwriting.* Liverpool, Light-Line Phonography Institute, 1888.

14. ————. *The Q's and A's of Shorthand Theory.* New York, The Gregg Publishing Company, 1924.

15. ————. "Rudiments of Light-Line," *The Light-Line Magazine*, I (January, 1893), p. 12.

16. ————. *Selections from the Story of Shorthand.* New York, The Gregg Publishing Company, undated but c. 1941.

17. ————. "The Story of Shorthand," *The Business Education World*, 1933-1941.

18. ———. *Teacher's Handbook to Gregg Speed Building, College Course*. New York, The Gregg Publishing Company, 1941.
19. ———. *The Teaching of Shorthand*. New York, The Gregg Publishing Company, 1916.
20. ———. *The Use of the Blackboard in Teaching Shorthand*. New York, The Gregg Publishing Company, 1928.
21. ———, Louis A. Leslie, and Charles E. Zoubek, *Gregg Speed Building Simplified*. New York, The Gregg Publishing Company, 1949.
22. Ingersoll, Walter E. (Editor). *The Book of the Silver Jubilee of Gregg Shorthand*. New York, The Gregg Publishing Company, 1913.
23. Leslie, Louis A. *Gregg Shorthand Manual for the Functional Method*. New York, The Gregg Publishing Company, 1936. (Two volumes)
24. ———. *The Teaching of Gregg Shorthand by the Functional Method*. New York, The Gregg Publishing Company, 1935.

5

SELECTED ILLUSTRATIONS FROM THE LIFE AND WORKS OF JOHN ROBERT GREGG

Dr. John Robert Gregg, 1867-1948.

John Robert Gregg, age ten, with sister
Fanny at Londonderry, Ireland. At ten he
studied Odell's adaptation of Taylor Shorthand.

George Gregg, father of John Robert Gregg.

John Robert Gregg at age twenty. The first book of Gregg Shorthand (then called *Light-Line Phonography*) was published at this time.

Imperial Chambers, Liverpool, the birthplace of Gregg Shorthand.

A reproduction of the first edition of Gregg Shorthand. This Liverpool edition, published on May 28, 1888, cost one shilling. There were only 500 copies of the original work printed.

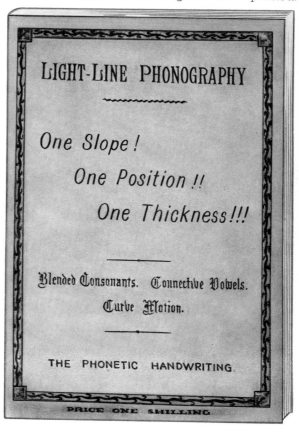

LIGHT-LINE PHONOGRAPHY

One Slope !

One Position !!

One Thickness !!!

Blended Consonants. Connective Vowels.
Curve Motion.

THE PHONETIC HANDWRITING.

PRICE ONE SHILLING

A reproduction of the first poster advertising Gregg Shorthand and Gregg's first school.

Gregg at twenty-five. The picture was taken at Liverpool.

First picture of Gregg in America, taken at Fitchburg, Massachusetts, in 1893 with two shipmates, Mackie (left) and Girvan (right).

Equitable Building, Boston, the first American home of Gregg Shorthand. The address was 150 Devonshire Street.

A flashlight picture of Gregg's first class in America at the Boys'
Institute of Industry, Boston, 1893.

Gregg's Shorthand.

A LIGHT-LINE PHONOGRAPHY
FOR THE MILLION.

ONE SLOPE!
ONE POSITION!!
ONE THICKNESS!!!
CONNECTIVE VOWELS!!!!

Part I —THE ELEMENTS.

PRICE 50 CENTS.

The first American edition of *Gregg's Short-hand*, of which this is a reproduction, was published in Boston on October 16, 1893. As in 1888, 500 copies were printed.

The Gregg School in the Tower Building, Chicago, was head-
quarters for three decades for methods of teaching Gregg Shorthand.

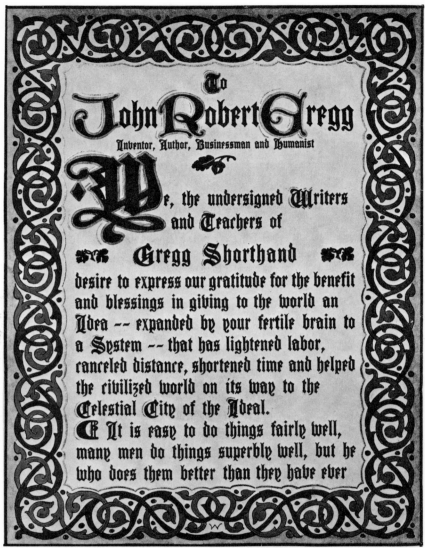

To

John Robert Gregg

Inventor, Author, Businessman and Humanist

We, the undersigned Writers
and Teachers of

Gregg Shorthand

desire to express our gratitude for the benefit
and blessings in giving to the world an
Idea -- expanded by your fertile brain to
a System -- that has lightened labor,
canceled distance, shortened time and helped
the civilized world on its way to the
Celestial City of the Ideal.
It is easy to do things fairly well,
many men do things superbly well, but he
who does them better than they have ever

Testimonial presented to John Robert Gregg on the occasion of the
Silver Jubilee of Gregg Shorthand in 1913. The convention marking

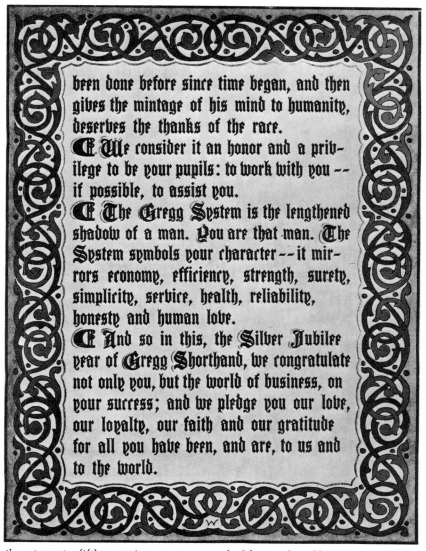

been done before since time began, and then gives the mintage of his mind to humanity, deserves the thanks of the race.

❧ We consider it an honor and a privilege to be your pupils: to work with you -- if possible, to assist you.

❧ The Gregg System is the lengthened shadow of a man. You are that man. The System symbols your character -- it mirrors economy, efficiency, strength, surety, simplicity, service, health, reliability, honesty and human love.

❧ And so in this, the Silver Jubilee year of Gregg Shorthand, we congratulate not only you, but the world of business, on your success; and we pledge you our love, our loyalty, our faith and our gratitude for all you have been, and are, to us and to the world.

the twenty-fifth anniversary was held at the Hotel LaSalle in Chicago.

John Robert Gregg in San Francisco in 1915 to attend the Panama Pacific International Exposition. The Gold Medal of Honor was awarded to Gregg Shorthand at the exposition.

An early issue of *The Gregg Writer*. The first issue was published in 1899. This magazine later became *Today's Secretary*.

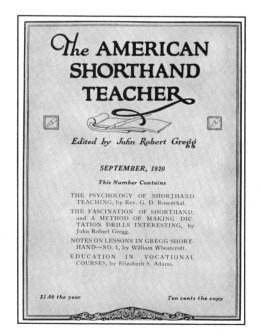

Another early Gregg magazine, *The American Shorthand Teacher*. In 1934, the name of the magazine was changed to *Business Education World*.

GREGG SHORTHAND

Frederick H. Gurtler, winner of Miner Medal in 1910.

Charles Lee Swem, World's Shorthand Champion, 1923-1924. He was also personal stenographer and official reporter to President Woodrow Wilson.

Swem taking down President Wilson's Flag Day address, June 14, 1915, on south steps of the Treasury Building.

CHAMPIONS

Albert Schneider, World's
Shorthand Champion, 1921.

Martin J. Dupraw, World's
Shorthand Champion, 1925-
1927.

Dupraw's trophies.

John Robert Gregg looking over the city of Dublin in 1928 from the top of the Independent Building.

Dr. Daniel L. Marsh, president of Boston University, congratulating John Robert Gregg after Doctor of Commercial Science Degree was conferred on him.

John Barrett, director general of the Pan-American Union, presenting Dr. Gregg with a testimonial signed by over a thousand Latin-American educators and others in twenty South American republics at a goodwill luncheon attended by 1,000 persons.

Boston's Mayor Curley presenting the "keys to the city" to Dr. Gregg.

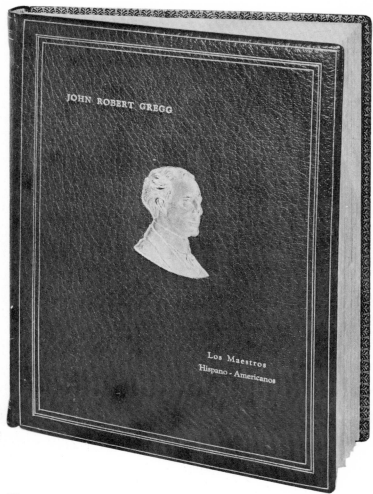

This memorial volume in Spanish was presented to Dr. Gregg at the Latin-American "Dia de Gregg" celebration in 1934 at the Waldorf-Astoria Hotel in New York City.

Dr. Gregg with Clarence Darrow at the convention of the National Commercial Teachers' Federation in 1934.

Dr. Fernando Batlle, consul general of the Dominican Republic, New York, thanking Dr. Gregg for his contribution to the development of business education in Latin America on behalf of educators throughout Latin America.

Dr. Gregg at his office on Madison Avenue, New York City, in 1935. With him are Louis A. Leslie (left), at that time editor of *The Gregg News Letter*, and Charles E. Zoubek (right), who was then associate editor.

Dr. Gregg receiving the "key to the city of Cleveland" from Mayor Burton.

The Ulster-Irish Society of New York presenting Dr. Gregg in 1936 with a gold medal for "Notable Service to the Nation." Mrs. Gregg is standing beside Dr. Gregg.

Rupert P. SoRelle, who was associated with the Gregg Publishing Company for many years and was vice-president from 1921 until his death in 1937.

Guy Stanley Fry, comptroller, secretary-treasurer, and then vice-president of the Gregg Publishing Company.

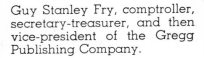

Henry J. Holm, for many years director of Gregg College in Chicago.

W. W. Lewis, who was head of the Shorthand Department of Gregg College.

Charles Zoubek, Louis Leslie, and Dr. Gregg at
Dr. Gregg's home in Connecticut.

Dr. and Mrs. Gregg with their two children at an office Christmas party.

Hubert A. Hagar, general manager and later vice-president of the Gregg Publishing Company, presenting Dr. Gregg with a diamond oval on Dr. Gregg's seventy-fifth birthday.

Dr. Paul S. Lomax, chairman, Department of Education, New York University School of Commerce, congratulating Dr. Gregg on the golden anniversary of Gregg Shorthand in the United States. Archibald A. Bowle, who was manager of the Latin-American Department of the Gregg Publishing Company, is standing in the front row at the left.

BRITISH CONSULATE GENERAL,
NEW YORK.

July 15, 1946

Dear Dr. Gregg,

I have today learned with great pleasure that His Majesty The King has been pleased to confer on you the King's Medal for Service in the Cause of Freedom for your valuable war time services.

Please allow me to offer you my heartiest congratulations on this honour which I know will be a source of immense satisfaction to your many friends.

Sir Francis Evans is at present on leave in the United Kingdom, but I know that he would wish me to convey to you on his behalf his sincerest good wishes and felicitations.

Yours sincerely,

A J Gardener.

A. J. Gardener
H. M. ~~Acting~~ Consul-General

Dr. John Robert Gregg,
Ulster Irish Society,
270 Madison Avenue,
New York

Letter sent to Dr. Gregg from the British Consulate General in New York City after Dr. Gregg had received the King's Medal for "Service in the Cause of Freedom."

Dr. Gregg presenting Hubert A. Hagar with a gold watch in recognition of Mr. Hagar's fortieth anniversary with the company.

One of the last photographs made of Dr. Gregg before his death in 1948.

Retirement dinner in honor of W. D. Wigent (center), who was manager of the Chicago office. With Mr. Wigent are Edward E. Booher (left), now president of McGraw-Hill Book Company, and Hubert A. Hagar (right).

November 10, 1962, was declared "Gregg Shorthand Day" in Boston in observance of the Diamond Jubilee of Gregg Shorthand. Deputy Mayor Henry A. Scagnoli (a Gregg Shorthand writer) welcomes to the city the publisher and the authors of *Gregg Shorthand*. Shown left to right are Robert E. Slaughter, senior vice-president, McGraw-Hill Book Company; Mr. Scagnoli; and coauthors Louis A. Leslie and Charles E. Zoubek.

Deputy Mayor Henry A. Scagnoli with coauthors Louis A. Leslie and Charles E. Zoubek. Mr. Leslie is holding a copy of *Gregg Shorthand, Diamond Jubilee Series.*

Dr. Paul S. Lomax, during the Diamond Jubilee celebration, speaks to over 500 persons at the Harvard Club of Boston on "John Robert Gregg: The Man and His Work—A Personal Recollection."

Henry J. Boer (right), manager of marketing services, attending the Diamond Jubilee celebration. Sitting next to Mr. Boer is the Reverend Frederick M. Meek, D.D., minister of Old South Church in Boston.

This painting of Dr. Gregg by John C. Johansen hangs over the fireplace in the John Robert Gregg Memorial Room of the National Arts Club, New York City. Dr. Gregg was a member of the National Arts Club for many years.

LIGHT-LINE PHONETIC HANDWRITING.

Reading Exercise.

[shorthand outlines]

Writing Exercise.

SELF-RELIANCE.

Don't rely on your friends. Don't rely upon your ancestors. Thousands have spent the prime of life in the vain hope of help from those whom they call friends, and thousands have starved because they had a rich father. Rely upon the good name which is made by your own exertions, and know that better than the best friend you can have is an unquestionable determination united with decision of character.

It is a fine thing in friendship to know when to be silent.

A page from the first Gregg Shorthand book, published in Liverpool, England, in 1888. Notice that a printed key was given for all the shorthand outlines. The shorthand, written by Gregg, was smaller than in later editions.

SELF-RELIANCE.

Don't rely on your friends. Don't rely upon your ancestors. Thousands have spent the prime of life in the vain hope of help from those whom they call friends, and thousands have starved because they had a rich father. Rely upon the name which is made by your own exertions, and know that better than the best friend you can have is an unquestionable determination united with decision of character.

READING EXERCISE.

A page from the second edition of Gregg Shorthand, published in Boston in 1893. A printed key was given for all shorthand outlines in the second edition also. The shorthand was written by Gregg.

SHORTHAND AS A MEANS OF MENTAL CULTURE.

[shorthand text]

A page from the third edition of Gregg Shorthand, published in Chicago in 1898. The shorthand for this edition was also written by Gregg.

SHORTHAND AS A MEANS OF MENTAL CULTURE.

A page from the fourth edition of Gregg Shorthand, published in Chicago in 1902. The shorthand for this edition was the last to be written by Gregg himself.

READING EXERCISE

A page from the fifth edition of Gregg Shorthand, published in 1916. The shorthand for the fifth edition was written by Mrs. Hubert A. Hagar. A great many brief forms and abbreviating devices were introduced.

A page from the Anniversary Edition, published in 1929. The Anniversary Edition was named in honor of the fortieth anniversary of the first publication of Gregg Shorthand. In this edition the shorthand was written by Mrs. Winifred Kenna Richmond.

READING AND WRITING PRACTICE

427. Opportunities in Business

, conjunction

, series

, as clause
organization

numerous
, parenthetical

intelligence
, conjunction

A page from *Gregg Shorthand Simplified*, published in 1949. This edition presented the first major simplification of the system, including a reduction of the memory load. Also, such features as marginal reminders were introduced. The shorthand was written by Charles Rader.

Reading and Writing Practice

498.

[Gregg shorthand outlines]

sug·ges'tions
de·rive'

serv'ic·ing
lo'cal
judg'ment

when

intro

intro

(136)

....

499.

yours
worn
worth'while'

if

INDEX

DATE DUE

DEC 1 9 1979		
JUN 2 3 1980 1981		
JUN 2 1981		
NOV 6 1981		
JUN 2 5 1986		
FEB 2 5 1987		
JUN 1 5 1989		
MAY 2 9 1990		
MAR 0 9 1991		